Why Men Won't Marry You

22 Truths Women Refuse to Hear – and 20 Ways to Fix It.

Copyright © 2026 Pinckney House
All rights reserved.

This publication is protected under the U.S. Copyright Act of 1976 and all other applicable international, federal, state, and local laws. No part of this book may be reproduced, stored in a retrieval system, or transmitted in any form or by any means, electronic, mechanical, photocopying, recording, scanning, or otherwise without the prior written permission of the copyright owner.

BOOK DISCLAIMER

This work should be considered satire and social commentary intended for discussion and analysis. This book discusses observed social patterns and outcomes. It does not claim all individuals behave the same, nor does it definitively assign intent or motive to every person within any group (in this case, women). These observations do describe how men *tend* to perceive behaviors, but these perceptions are in no means, absolute.

Written by: Kelly Ruff
Prepared for Publication by: Kali Pinckney & Team
Published by: Pinckney House

ISBN 13: 979-8-218-91018-1

Author's Note

In *Why Men Won't Marry You*, we examine why men are walking away from modern marriage. This book is not here to tell you what you want to hear. It is to explore what you NEED to hear. It's not about hating women. It's about honesty. Our goal is to answer the questions that many modern women are asking. This book exposes why men are avoiding modern marriage, points out what women refuse to see about their own behavior, choices, and expectations.

Some parts may sting a bit, but they're supposed to. Because the truth about love, loyalty, and peace has been buried under ego and entitlement for far too long. Yes, I use some satire, but do not doubt that men agree with it.

You can choose to believe that it is just satire, but good satire is based on truth. Read it with an open mind, especially if you hope to get married one day. Believe it or not, this information is how men think. If you accept this information, you might actually understand what men have been trying to tell you all along.

If you want to be a wife, obviously, you must understand a man's perspective...

— Kelly Ruff

Table of Contents

How We Got Here! 2
The Curse of Eve 5
The 22 Truths 10
Legal and Financial Hazards 14
Behavioral Red Flags 33
Your Personality Flaws 48
Fitness and Body Counts 63
Cultural and Societal Influences 72
What Does This All Mean for You? 116
Why Would a Man Choose You? 125
20 Tenets to Marriage 137
The End Is Near 183
The Final Verdict 192

> "You can ignore reality, but you cannot ignore the consequences of ignoring reality."
>
> -Ayn Rand

Kelly Ruff

How We Got Here!

• • •

Let us not sugarcoat it: marriage is in trouble. And if you want to be a wife, you need to hear why.

If marriage were a business deal, no smart man would sign the contract. The risks are obvious, the penalties are brutal, and the return on investment keeps shrinking. Yet women still act surprised, as if men suddenly forgot how to love. That is not the case. Men remember love. They remember loyalty. What they no longer see is value in a system that strips both away the moment a woman decides she is not happy.

This book exists for one purpose. To tell the truth, reason by reason, without excuses. Some of what you read will sting. Some of it will make you angry. But all of it reflects the struggles men live through in silence. These reasons are not complaints or theories. They are patterns that appear in homes, bedrooms, courts, workplaces, and everywhere modern relationships fall apart.

The concepts in these pages explain why men hesitate. Why they pause, why they pull back before proposing, and why they choose freedom over a promise that no longer feels safe.

Read carefully. What follows is the blueprint men already know. It is the map of why they walk away from marriage and why they no longer line up for a game they cannot win. Each truth reveals something about modern women that culture refuses to confront. Each truth exposes the gap between what women believe they offer and what men experience.

You can ignore reality, but the consequences will always catch up with you. That is why this all should matter to you as a woman. It shows the patterns that break men, the behaviors that destroy respect, and the attitudes that turn relationships into battlefields.

If you truly want to understand why men hesitate, this is where you begin. Not in your feelings, not in what you think you deserve, and not in the fantasy of what marriage used to be. You start with the truth. You start with what men have been too tired to say out loud. You start with twenty-two reasons why men will not marry you.

Before you can understand these 22 truths, you must understand the root cause. Modern behavior did not appear out of nowhere. It came from a story as old as humanity itself. To see the patterns in women today, you have to look at where the pattern originated. That story starts long before dating apps, divorce courts, and social media. It begins with Eve.

Why Men Won't Marry You

The Curse of Eve

• • •

Once upon a time, there was a woman named Eve. She lived in a perfect garden with her man, Adam. He took care of her and protected her from all dangers. He hunted for her, built her shelter, and made sure her life was nothing but peaceful.

The garden they lived in was heaven on Earth. Every sunrise painted the sky bright gold, while the rivers were so clean you could dip your hand in and pull out a rainbow-colored fish for dinner. The sound of the water flowing was like a choir singing across the banks.

Fruit trees leaned over perfectly to allow Adam and Eve to pick their sweet, succulent, fruity deliciousness. The air was so crisp and pure that it felt like breathing in pure peppermint patties. Beneath her feet, the grass was like soft emerald velvet. And Eve, beautiful Eve, walked through it all without a stitch of clothing, happy and unashamed.

Her man, Adam, was the reason she even existed. He loved her and would have done anything to make sure she had it all. And she did. No hunger. No pain. No strife and no fear. No mosquitoes, no sickness, no wrinkles. Her body was flawless and untouched by the ravages of stress or time. She lived a life that every woman since has secretly envied.

But for Eve, it still wasn't enough.

The story of Eve is not just a religious tale. It is the oldest explanation of human behavior that still plays out in modern relationships. Whether you believe the story literally or see it as symbolism, the lesson is the same. A woman was given everything. Peace. Security. Provision. A good man who trusted her without hesitation. She had the easiest life imaginable, and it still was not enough. One temptation. One whispered idea that she deserved more. One moment of entitlement. That was all it took to ruin everything.

Adam paid the price for a choice he did not make. That pattern never disappeared. Men still carry the consequences of a woman's decisions. Men still get blamed for the fallout. They still try to protect, provide, and stay loyal, even when the woman next to them reaches for something she has no business touching.

Eve did not fall because she was evil. She fell because she was convinced she deserved more than what she already had. She had paradise but wanted power. She had stability but craved control. She had peace but wanted a thrill. And when it all fell apart, she did not take the punishment alone. Adam took it with her.

This is something women do not like to acknowledge. Women create the storm, and men walk through the consequences. Women follow their feelings, and men pay the cost. The curse was not fruit. It was the refusal to take responsibility.

You see it today in modern marriages. A woman destroys her own home through betrayal, entitlement, or selfish choices, and the man is expected to endure the damage without complaint. She breaks the relationship, and he pays for child support. She files for divorce, and he loses his house. She grows bored, and he becomes the villain. Women still chase the thrill. Men still carry the burden.

The story of Eve is not an attack on women. It is a reminder that human nature has not changed. The patterns are ancient, and the consequences are predictable. If a woman does not understand this truth, she will repeat it. If she refuses to confront her own nature, she will blame every failed relationship on the man. If she ignores the mistake that led to the downfall, she will keep falling.

To understand the reasons men avoid marriage, you must understand the pattern that has existed since the beginning. Women want more until they lose everything, and men are left to rebuild the ruins.

This is the curse of Eve.
And this is where the truth begins.

"When you're accustomed to privilege, equality feels like oppression."

-Author Unknown

The story of Eve explains the pattern, while the world you live in reveals the consequences. What comes next explains the reality men face today. These truths are not theories or rare events. They are the everyday experiences that shape how men see commitment, marriage, and risk. The curse created the blueprint, but modern behavior filled in every detail.

If you want to understand why men hesitate, you must see what they see. If you want to understand why men avoid marriage, you must understand the 22 Truths that define their choices.

This is where the patterns become clear and the excuses fall apart. This is where the truth speaks louder than feelings.

Now we begin.

The 22 Truths

• • •

The 22 Truths in this book are not theories or complaints. They come from patterns that repeat in modern relationships, whether anyone wants to admit it or not. Men see them. Women feel them. Culture ignores them. If a man has not lived through these truths himself, he knows men who have.

Truth does not need approval. It does not disappear because someone gets offended. A truth simply reveals what is real. These 22 Truths highlight why modern men hesitate to commit and why marriage feels like a gamble they are no longer willing to take.

Every man who reads this list will instantly recognize the accuracy. Every woman who feels anger rising inside her is reacting to something she knows applies to her or to the women she defends. That discomfort is the first sign that these truths matter. Denial is the last privilege you lose before change begins.

These truths were not created to shame women. They exist because men have spent years carrying the fallout of choices they did not make. They have watched the legal system, modern culture, and relationship expectations twist into something that demands everything from men while offering extraordinarily little in return. Men have learned that love alone is not enough when the person they choose believes accountability is optional.

Each truth exposes a pattern that weakens relationships. Some are emotional. Some are behavioral. Some are financial. Some are the result of cultural conditioning. Together, they form the unfortunate image men see when they think about marriage today.

As you read, it's natural to feel a bit defensive. You may feel judged, exposed, or dare I say, triggered. That is normal. Growth rarely feels good at the beginning. Pay attention to what stings your ego. That is the part that needs honesty.

These 22 Truths explain why good men withdraw, why loyal men stop trying, and why honorable men choose freedom over a commitment that feels rigged. They reveal what men have been too tired to say and what women have been encouraged to overlook.

The risks associated with marriage are obvious. If it fails, it could take damn near a decade to recover emotionally and financially, if recovery is possible. Yet women still act confused, as if men suddenly have forgotten how to love. That is not the case. Men remember love. They remember loyalty. What they no longer see is any value in a system designed to strip them of both.

The reasons are not random complaints. They are patterns, repeated across homes, courts, workplaces, and bedrooms. They are the dealbreakers men do not say out loud but act on when they choose to stay single. And if you genuinely want to understand why men hesitate, this is where you start.

So read carefully. What follows is the blueprint of why men are no longer lining up for marriage.

Legal and Financial Hazards

• • •

When a man marries, he does not just marry the woman. He marries the government. He signs a legal contract that can take everything he has built and hand it over to someone who may one day decide she is no longer happy. Men do not avoid marriage because they fear commitment. They avoid it because the moment vows are exchanged, the law stops being neutral. If the marriage fails, the courts, the lawyers, the state, and the woman he married all get a piece of him.

Marriage changes women too. Before the ring, she meets him halfway. After the ring, she knows she does not have to. The system gives her a soft landing no matter how high she jumps. Even when at fault, she can walk away with his house, his paycheck, his time, and his peace, and society will call it empowerment.

The statistics are clear: data from Census Bureau, CDC, and Pew Research data show that almost half of marriages end in divorce. Women initiate the majority of them and receive custody and financial support in most cases. While the percentages shift slightly each year, the pattern never changes. Men lose, and the system wins.

This is why modern men hesitate. It is not fear of love. It is fear of losing everything for it.

Who makes more money? If it is him, the answer is simple. He just became her ATM. Alimony comes out of his pocket, child support becomes his responsibility, and he foots her legal fees. Half his retirement becomes hers, and the house becomes hers. Even the family dog's future depends on how emotional she gets in court. If he points out her flaws, he becomes labeled as angry, controlling, or abusive in the eyes of the court. Her tears are not just feelings. They are evidence.

Divorce becomes a ritual of humiliation. He sits with lawyers, hands over documents, fights over furniture, writes checks, and apologizes for things he did not do. He pays his lawyer and indirectly finances hers through assets she now controls. He is funding his own mugging.

The damage does not stop at his bank account. His friendships suffer, his family is pulled into the fight, and his children become leverage. His peace evaporates. As his credit collapses. His confidence disappears, and even therapy becomes another bill he pays so he can explain why everything hurts.

Meanwhile, she cries in court and posts vacation photos a month later. She receives sympathy, support, and praise for finding herself. He gets a thin-walled apartment, a mattress on the floor, and two boxes labeled "Dad's stuff." He becomes the punchline in a story he paid to write.

And for her, the payments keep coming. He pays until she remarries, which she has no incentive to do. Why marry again when she can keep the monthly income? He pays until the kids are grown, unless she returns to court for college expenses. Some men pay until they die, and yes, she may also expect some of his life insurance to secure her stream of income... *"for the kids."*

If he paid for the wedding, he will definitely pay for the divorce. He ends up paying twice. Add in the emotional, financial, and legal costs and this deal doesn't look so good. And for what? A few years of consistent sex, a stack of photos, and a lifetime of regret? Divorce is not just the end of a relationship. It is proof that the system was never designed to protect the man. It rewards whoever cries the loudest while holding the kids.

Marriage is expensive. Divorce is catastrophic. The system is not broken. It works exactly as designed. Against him. This is why men calculate risk long before they propose. They know the law favors her at every turn. They know one signature can erase everything they spent their lives building.

This is the first truth men grow to understand. And this is why they think twice before handing their future to someone who may one day call a lawyer.

Now, we look at the truths that follow.

"Men are not the problem. The choices of women are the problem. You control access to sex. Men control access to relationships and marriage."

-Kevin Samuels

Truth #1 – Marriage Is a Rigged Deal

Women know the law is on their side, so do not pretend otherwise. You could burn a man's clothes, key his car, and insult his mother, and nothing would happen nine times out of ten. But if he raises his voice at you above a whisper, the world reacts as if he is a threat to humanity. Out comes the restraining order. Out comes the court summons. Out comes the weekend-only custody schedule. He is pushed into a one-bedroom apartment and supervised visits while she walks away with the house, the car, and a round of applause from her friends.

This is why men are backing out of marriage. They see the playbook. If a woman cheats, she still gets child support, alimony, and the moral high ground. If a man cheats, he gets crucified socially, financially, and publicly. The system lacks gender equality. As such, it is legalized extraction. Men have figured this out faster than women want to admit.

A woman must recognize that a man who marries her is trying to build something. A future. A family. A life together. He provides the stability **you say** you want. He builds a home, provides the support, and generally improves your living conditions. Then one day you decide you are unfulfilled and you file for divorce. He loses everything except the responsibility. He finances a family he no longer leads. He pays your bills while eating microwave dinners on a folding chair. Courts do not care about loyalty or vows. They care about paperwork. And the paperwork always favors her.

That is not a partnership or equality. That is a man working himself into the ground for a person who no longer carry his last name. There is a word for that: slave.

The system does not simply allow women to leave. It rewards them for leaving. If she breaks her vows; he still pays the bills. If she shatters the home; he still funds her lifestyle. That is not marriage. That is a subscription that charges him forever.

' And Prenups Are a Joke

Prenuptial agreements were supposed to protect men from women who saw marriage as a financial opportunity; or from wives who detonate a marriage because, just like Eve, they want "more". Once seen as a form of insurance, today, they are just decoration. Judges toss them aside like expired coupons the moment a wife's eyes water, proclaiming that she didn't understand what signing it meant.

The only prenups that are rock-solid guaranteed are the ones the wife initiates, that are thoroughly reviewed by her lawyers, and discussed with his lawyers before a marriage. Other than that, a judge will ignore it if he or she believes it does not benefit the wife. 'And if the judge is a woman... God help the husband!

The wife could be recorded signing the prenup while holding a Bible in one hand and yelling she understands the prenup, and a judge would still claim she did not fully understand what she was giving up. It is nonsense. Prenups no longer provide protection. They provide false confidence, legal bills, and wasted time.

Even when a prenup holds, the man is still exposed. Alimony, asset division, court fees, and strategic accusations can drain him dry. A prenup does not shield his home, his retirement, or his sanity. It protects nothing except her smile in divorce court.

Men have learned the truth. The prenup will not save you. It is not a shield. It is not armor. It is a participation trophy you burn for heat while she drives away in the car you pay for.

For modern men, the prenup has transformed into a cruel joke, and the punchline is always expensive.

Truth #2 – Government Supports Women

Men are not blind. They see exactly how the system works. They watch women cheat, lie, drain bank accounts, destroy property, and to make it all worse, they make videos and post it all to the internet, like it's a job. But the government doesn't care about truth, it treats the man like he is the problem in the marriage.

A woman can detonate the relationship like a grenade, walk into court as the victim, and walk out with a check, a house, and a legally enforced slice of his future. More and more men are learning that staying single, is better than volunteering for a state-sponsored robbery.

Women claim they want equality, but everyone knows the truth. The courts are their safety net, and the laws protect them. The system believes them even when they are the ones who are obviously the problem. If he raises his voice, he is dangerous. If she throws furniture, she is emotional. That is not equality. That is government-backed gaslighting.

The numbers prove it. Most divorces are filed by women. Men get blindsided, coming home from work to find the locks changed, the bank account empty, and the papers already filed. By the time he realizes what happened, she is halfway out the door with his future under her arm.

Men are not intimidated by women; they are intimidated by the risk of being punished by a government that does not care about them.

He'll Lose Half of Everything

A man avoids marriage because it is not just a risk to his heart. It is a gamble with every asset he has ever built. His house, his car, his retirement, his business, and his savings are on the line the moment she says, "I am not happy." The average divorced man loses half of what he owns and can gain decades of debt. He'll end up in a small rental apartment with a folding chair and an air fryer while she decorates the marital home he paid for, and she refuses to leave.

It does not matter who earned the money or who worked the hours, took the risks, or built the business. The moment divorce papers are served, She's claiming everything is a "shared asset". Her name will appear on everything he created. She suddenly discovers a deep passion for self-care, spiritual retreats, and lawyers with polished names like, Chadwick and Steele. His net worth becomes a joke, his credit collapses, and his friends shake their heads, muttering, "You should have seen it coming."

This is why men hesitate. The only thing more expensive than a wife, is an ex-wife with a lawyer and an attitude.

He Pays Long Before Marriage Even Starts

Men fear losing everything in divorce, but also the costs that start long before the wedding. Women brag about being strong, independent women... until the check arrives. Suddenly, it is 1952 all over again, and he better pay for dinner, drinks, nails, hair, and transportation or he is not a "real man."

He pays for the first date, the second, the third, the brunch, the trip, and sometimes the vacation before he even knows her last name. Women bring expectations like royalty and treat contribution like an insult. Men are tired of paying for auditions when the reward is more bills and less gratitude.

The Price Only Increases Inside Marriage

Marriage arrives and he pays for the ring. In modern times, he pays for the wedding, the honeymoon, the mortgage, the kids, and the lifestyle. If it all collapses, he keeps paying while she finds herself and updates her social media. She wants equality, but he is still the financial engine while she shouts empowerment with a mouth full of the steak he bought.

Men may be a little slow sometimes, but they are not stupid. They believe in romance and love, but they are coming to grips with reality. Marriage is not a partnership. It is not about fairness. It is a subscription service with no cancellation policy. Every year the cost goes up. Every year the value goes down.

Truth #3 – Paternity Fraud and Other People's Kids

There is only one betrayal that cuts deeper than cheating to a man.

Paternity Fraud! That is the ultimate betrayal.

Women love to say that men cheat too, and yes, men cheat. But there is one kind of cheating only women can commit. A woman can become pregnant by another man and convince someone else to raise that child. A man cannot lie about who the mother is, while a woman can lie about who the father is. She will then use the legal system to force him into eighteen years of financial slavery. That is not an accident. That is fraud with a smile.

Although findings can vary from one study to another, it is estimated that 5–15% of paternity tests reveal that the man identified as the father was not actually the biological father. It is worth noting that paternity tests are normally conducted when there is some pre-existing question about paternity, but that also suggests that the actual percentage might be higher if you were to test a larger sample of presumed fathers.

Thanks to DNA tests from companies like 23andMe, Ancestry, and even drugstore swabs, there is no excuse. A man deserves to know if his children are genetically his. Modern empowerment talks a lot about honesty, but rarely about paternity. Men cannot lie about biology. Women can. And when that power is weaponized to trap a man with another man's baby, it destroys everything. It shakes a man's identity, his trust, and the foundation of family itself.

If he discovers the truth too late, he is stuck. Emotionally, financially, and legally, he is

locked in. In many states, if he signed the birth certificate, he is obligated regardless of the DNA results. Courts do not care about biology. They care about paperwork. That is not love. That is deception in yoga pants. And it is one of the reasons men are walking away from the altar.

Your Kids Are Not His Responsibility.

Another hazard men face is simpler but just as serious. You have children with another man and expect the next man to play stepdad as if it were charity work. You call it a blended family. He calls it raising someone else's children while being blamed for everything. And somehow, you act like you are doing him a favor.

Let us be honest. Most men do not dream of raising another man's kids. Especially not when those same children worship their absentee father while treating the man who buys the groceries, pays the rent, and drives them to practice like he is Brad from payroll. You expect him to invest time, money, energy, and love into children who are not biologically his. At the same time, he has to navigate the ex, manage drama, and receive little to no appreciation. That is not a relationship. That is a hostage situation with lunchboxes.

Life happens. Relationships fail. Kids end up in the middle. That does not change the truth. Being a single mother lowers your value in the dating market. Not because you are a bad person, but because you bring responsibilities most men never signed up for. Expecting a man to step in as a bonus dad simply because you are attractive and tired of being alone is not realistic. It is delusional.

Can it work? Yes, but the deal has to be exceptional. A man will consider a single mother only when she brings peace, loyalty, femininity, gratitude, and absolute stability. The more children you have, the higher the climb. Each child adds another layer of complexity. It serves as another reminder that your life comes with built-in chaos.

If you do land a good man, understand the significance of that. He is doing you a favor, not the other way around. Respect his sacrifice. Appreciate what he risks. And keep your children under control.

If you are a single mother wondering why dating feels impossible, proclaiming that sometimes **real women** have gone through stuff. Well, the truth is that men are not intimidated by a real woman. They are avoiding taking on another man's responsibilities. Your kids and the choices that created your situation make a marriage with you seem riskier... *To the man* who wants to date you. 'And the more children you have, the more risk he sees.

And the more kiddos, by different fathers, the more risk still! Who is marrying women with 3 or 4 kids, by 3 or 4 different fathers. That is diabolical! No self-respecting man does this.

Truth #4 – Men's Souls Get Destroyed

Women think heartbreak hurts them. They have no idea what it does to a man. A failed relationship shatters your feelings, but a failed marriage ruins his entire life. Try losing your home, your kids, your money, your purpose, and your peace of mind, all while being told to "Man Up." When relationships collapse, men do not just get angry and depressed. They get destroyed. Emotionally. Financially. Legally. Socially.

You never see the wreckage because men are expected to suffer in silence. You leave; he pays. You cheat; he apologizes. You lie; he is expected to understand. And when he finally breaks under the weight of it all, you call him unstable. No one asks what he lost. No one asks if he is okay. His pain is invisible because the world measures men by what they provide and produce, not by what they feel.

Men die inside quietly. A man who once laughed easily, now stares into nothing, hollowed out by obligations he never agreed to carry alone. His drive fades. His energy drains. His spirit erodes. Nights that once held dreams now hold dread, because he does not see hope an end to his circumstances. Even his children feel distant because nothing in his life feels like his anymore. He becomes a ghost of the man he once was.

Marriage does not just hurt men. It bleeds them dry until nothing is left. The destruction goes deeper than money or property. It touches their purpose. Their pride. Their identity. Every sacrifice is ignored, every effort minimized, and every failure magnified. What once made him proud, like providing and protecting, becomes ammunition for criticism. His victories are dismissed, while his struggles are mocked. Instead of being seen as a contributor, his existence becomes a burden.

And society cheers while it happens. His downfall becomes entertainment. His suffering becomes a meme. Men are mocked for caring, punished for failing, and ridiculed for breaking. The emptiness does not stay at home. It follows him to work, into friendships, and into his health. Stress crushes him from the inside, shaving years off his life.

This is why men are growing contempt toward the institution of marriage. They are afraid of becoming hollow and waking up one day to realize that the last piece of their soul was signed away on a marriage certificate. They are choosing to protect what is left of themselves.

So let us say he survives the financial destruction, the paternity roulette, and the slow draining of his spirit. Maybe he convinces himself he can handle it, that he thinks he is tougher than the men before him. Good for him. What he does not realize is that the hardest part is not the court, the state, or the child support office. It is the person waiting for him at home. The real danger comes from betrayal, and unresolved trauma.

Marriage is Too Much of a Gamble

Marriage is the worst gamble a man can make. At least when you gamble in Las Vegas and lose everything, they hand you a free drink and pretend to feel bad. Marriage offers no such courtesy. You walk in believing you hit the jackpot. She laughs at your jokes, tolerates your playlist, and she notices and overlooks the lack of furniture and food in your house. You think this girl might be different. Spoiler: She is not!

Her married perspective will shift. His jokes will stop being funny. His playlist will become immature. And if the marriage fails, He will not walk away as he walked in. He will walk away broke, bruised, and legally obligated to keep funding her lifestyle while she starts her "healing journey" on social media.

Marriage is like betting your life savings on one hand while the dealer changes the rules whenever she wants. There are no cocktails and no apology. There is only the bill. That is not love. That is Russian roulette with a legal contract. Men are expected to risk everything for a prize that might never pay out. The longer they stay in the game, the worse the odds become. Every year adds another zero to the risk while the reward shrinks.

Women brag about loyalty until they are not happy. Then it is off to the courthouse like it is a spa appointment. It is not random that most divorces are initiated by the wife.

The same woman who promised forever will file papers the moment she thinks she can do better. Men see this. They see that loyalty has an expiration date triggered by boredom, resentment, or a wealthier option. What was sold as a lifelong vow becomes a temporary contract that can be shredded the moment it becomes inconvenient.

The fallout is brutal. Divorce does not just end the relationship. It financially destroys him. He pays for the kids, the house, her lifestyle, and his sad little apartment. Even if she cheated, he still pays. That is why men stay trapped or wait until the kids are grown before leaving. They know the game is rigged. They know the house always wins.

The smartest men step away before they ever sit down. The rest eventually realized the jackpot never existed.

"Men do not fear women. They fear what loving the wrong one turns them into."

Behavioral Red Flags

• • •

When men talk about why they avoid marriage, they point to one thing before anything else. Behavior. Not beauty. Not age. Not money. Behavior. Looks may attract him, but how a woman acts determines whether he stays. A man can handle stress and demanding times. What he will not do is sign up for a lifetime of disrespect, nagging, chaos, manipulation, or emotional warfare. These are the habits that turn love into labor and turn relationships into punishment.

Modern women are told that their behavior does not matter, that a man should accept anything she does as long as she feels justified. Men no longer believe that. They pay attention to how a woman speaks, how she argues, how she handles pressure, and how she treats people who cannot benefit her. If he sees constant drama, loud outbursts, or emotional games, he knows exactly what life with her will be like. And it will not be peaceful.

Behavior is the daily reality of a relationship. You can fake charm for a few weeks, but you cannot fake the way you communicate, the way you listen, or the way you show respect. If your behavior destroys a man's peaceful existence, he will protect himself by keeping his distance. A woman's actions either build a home or burn it down, and men see that long before a proposal is ever considered.

The worst thing that can happen to a man who has little experience with women is "falling in love" with someone emotional or chaotic. He does not have the history or insight of what to look for in a woman. Without a clearer perspective, he can still confuse love with crazy.

This section exposes the behavioral patterns that push men away from marriage. Each one is a red flag that tells him he will be trading his freedom for conflict, disrespect, or chaos he never agreed to. Men are not searching for perfection. They are searching for peace. Peace is impossible when a woman refuses to control her behavior.

Truth #5 – Cheating & Rosters

Let us not pretend the roster does not exist. Maybe it is not written on paper, but it is alive in your phone, your DMs, and in the background of your life. You call them friends, work buddies, or people you have known forever. He calls them what they are. Standby options. You may be dating one man, but you have three on the bench, two stretching on the sideline, and one texting you every Friday night asking if you are up.

Men are not stupid. They see the game. When you say you need space, he knows you are checking your Friend Zone. You will swear you are loyal until you feel ignored for a weekend. Suddenly, the man who was like a brother is holding your hand at brunch. When you get caught, you shrug and say it just happened. As if betrayal is an accident of gravity instead of a decision you prepared for the moment you left the door cracked open.

Having a roster is a giant red flag. A man might sleep with you, but marry you? Not a chance. He knows he is not competing with your ex. He is competing with your entire squad. That is not commitment. That is playoffs in your DMs.

Ghosts of Past Trauma

Women love to say men avoid commitment because they are emotionally unavailable. Wrong. Men remember. They remember how they were treated before. They remember the woman who drained their energy, their money, their dignity, and their hope. They are not avoiding you. They are avoiding what you might remind them of.

Every man has that one ghost from his past. The woman he cared for, but who broke him in ways he never spoke about. Not only financially, but emotionally and spiritually. She did not just hurt him. She used him and taught him a lesson he would never forget.

Because of that ghost, every new woman is scanned like luggage at an airport. He is on the lookout for hidden explosives: passive aggression, emotional games, inconsistent communication, and the weaponized phrase, "I'm fine." You are not competing with other women. You are competing with the damage left behind by the women who came before you.

That ghost whispers in his ear every time you roll your eyes, raise your voice, or treat him like a backup plan. It reminds him not to fall for the same tricks twice. It warns him that love can become debt, that loyalty can become leverage, and that giving too much can destroy a man from the inside out.

If you cannot offer more peace than the ghost, do not be surprised when he chooses the memory over the marriage. Men do not fear commitment. They fear déjà vu. They refuse to buy the same ticket to the same painful show for a second time.

A CASE STUDY: *Antonio & Rosa*

After seventy-seven years of marriage, ninety-nine-year-old Antonio C. from Italy filed for divorce from his ninety-six-year-old wife, Rosa C. The shock stemmed from a discovery just before Christmas when he found a stack of letters tucked away in an old chest of drawers, revealing a love affair Rosa had kept hidden for over sixty years. The previously private correspondence changed everything.

When Antonio confronted Rosa, she reportedly admitted to the long-ago affair. Despite their decades together and their five children, twelve grandchildren, and one great-grandchild, Antonio insisted that the disclosure altered the terms of their relationship. According to the reports, he felt the marriage contract had been breached by secrecy and chose to seek a legal end to the union.

The case stands as a dramatic illustration of how even the longest commitments can unravel when underlying trust is shaken. What appears as a lifetime of loyalty may conceal unresolved choice, hidden options, or unspoken conditions. For the purposes of this manuscript-wide topic, their story highlights a key point: long-term relationships are not immune to the same rules of value, standards, and risk as newer contracts of commitment.

Truth #6 – You're Not a Prize

Women have been told for decades that they are the prize simply for existing, as if showing up with makeup, Wi-Fi, and a pulse is enough to earn a man's lifelong devotion. But a prize is not declared. A prize is earned. Men do not stay because a woman insists she is special. They stay when she brings peace, loyalty, warmth, and real value. If your greatest offering is presence, you are not the prize. You are a participant.

The real prize is the person who makes life better, not harder. Men invest in women who add joy, respect, and calm, not stress, conflict, and expense. If you believe you are the ultimate catch, ask yourself something uncomfortable. Would you date you? Would you compete for you? Would you make sacrifices for a woman with your attitude, your habits, and your emotional discipline? A true prize does not yell its worth. It demonstrates its value through consistency, humility, and behavior.

Instead, many women walk into the world anticipating theme music to start playing and the crowd parting in reverence. They expect men to chase, compete, and worship their existence. Newsflash. You are not a goddess, and men are not your disciples. No one is composing poetry about your iced coffee order or your curated cell phone selfies. That is not confidence. That is entitlement dipped in lip gloss.

Then comes the career flex. Women assume that degrees, job titles, and salaries are irresistible to men. They are not. Men do not marry résumés. They marry character. Your income does not make you more nurturing, peaceful, or easier to live with. It simply means you can pay your own bills, which is the minimum requirement for adulthood. If you brag about your achievements while ignoring your attitude, you are not raising your value. You are lowering it.

A man will marry a barista, a receptionist, or a waitress if she is feminine, loyal, and brings peace. Meanwhile, your "boss babe" energy creates more competition than comfort. Men are not looking for a rival. They are not impressed by your LinkedIn profile. The sooner you accept that, the sooner you'll understand why acting like the prize has produced the opposite effect.

Here is the truth. If you demand a pedestal, do not be surprised when men walk away. A man does not sign up to worship anyone. He signs up for a role-based partnership. If you cannot offer that, you are not the prize at all.

Double Standards

Women create rules for the men they do not want and break those rules for the men they do want.

That single sentence explains almost everything wrong with modern dating. Women love to list their non negotiables like they are hiring a CEO with a six-pack. He must be tall, wealthy, emotionally intelligent, stylish, confident, assertive, attentive, ambitious, respectful, funny, mentally stable, physically fit, financially secure, and spiritually grounded. In other words, Prince Charming with a high limit, Black Card to flex his credit score.

Meanwhile, what does she bring? A shaky attitude, unresolved trauma, inconsistent habits, and a gym membership used once a season. Yet she expects a king to kneel at her door.

If women had to meet the same standards they demand from men, most would be single for life. They want a man who is fit but refuse to step foot in a gym. They want a man who is financially stable while drowning in credit card debt. They want a man who communicates well yet has emotional reactions that require subtitles.

Men are expected to be providers, protectors, comedians, therapists, and life coaches, all while women expect praise for simply existing. And when an unwanted man approaches them, the rules come out. No short men. No broke men. No roommates. No imperfections.

But when a man that a woman actually desires shows interest, suddenly all the rules disappear. Height does not matter. Debt becomes irrelevant. Standards do not count. They convince themselves he is working on himself or has potential, because attraction overrides every "principle" she claimed was nonnegotiable.

This is the hypocrisy men see, which is why they are done jumping through hoops. They realize the rules were never rules. They were excuses to reject the men that women were never attracted to in the first place.

If women had to date themselves using the same checklist they apply to men, they would swipe left on their own profiles halfway through. And if they held themselves to the same standards they demand, many would finally understand how average they truly are.

Truth #7 – You're Abusive, Yet You Play the Victim

Here is the part women never want to hear. A man will not marry you because one fake accusation can destroy his entire life. The word "abuse" is a weapon. The moment you say it, people imagine a man hurting a woman. But the truth is that women abuse men at higher rates than anyone wants to admit. Not just verbally or emotionally, but physically too.

Society loves to say real men do not hit women. Somehow, the world forgets the other half of that sentence. Real women should not hit men. Yet many do. Women slap, shove, throw objects, scream, hit, and brag about "getting in his face." They call it passion or emotion. But if a man did half of what women do during an argument, he would be in handcuffs before the echo faded.

A woman can scratch, punch, slap, or throw things, and everyone still rushes to protect her. The police, the courts, her friends, and even his family will assume he is the threat simply because he is a man. Meanwhile, he stands there as a human punching bag with no way to defend himself. If he so much as raises his voice, it becomes toxic masculinity, and the next stop is the courtroom.

And physical abuse is only part of the story. Many women walk around with a permanent chip on their shoulder. They expect disappointment, assume the worst, and treat resentment like a daily vitamin. They are still angry at their exes, their fathers, their last situationships, and now every new man has to pay for wounds he did not create. That is not a relationship. That is a courtroom drama where he is guilty before the trial starts.

Men feel this. You do not radiate warmth, softness, or peace. You radiate hostility, spite, and emotional volatility. You are defensive, combative, and draining. Then you wonder why men disappear. No man signs up to be punished for the sins of men he has never met. No man wants to build a future with someone still trying to win arguments from three relationships ago.

The truth is simple. You are not fighting him. You are fighting ghosts. In the end, the only person left to argue with will be yourself. Men see the battle forming long before you do. That is why they walk away before signing their name onto a conflict that never ends.

Entitlement

After all that, you would think the man deserves a medal for staying. Instead, this is when the personality circus arrives. If you are not playing the victim, you are putting on a crown and demanding to be treated like royalty while offering nothing in return. This is when men realize the issue is not just behavior. It is the mindset. The entitlement, the blame shifting, the delusion about what men actually want. It is like touring a dream home and finding out the foundation is cracked, the wiring is dangerous, and the neighborhood is a hazard. Welcome to the personality flaw section.

Women have been told they are empowered, but somewhere along the way, the message got twisted. Empowerment became entitlement. Many women believe that having a job, an apartment, and a Pinterest board means they deserve any man they want. No man owes you a date, a ring, or devotion. He is not even obligated to give you attention. Existing does not entitle you to a high-value man.

You call yourself a boss while still expecting men to pay for everything. You preach independence until the check arrives, then suddenly tradition sounds amazing. Empowerment once meant discipline, accountability, and self-respect. These days, it often means reckless actions paired with the expectation that a man will clean up the mess.

This new version of entitlement is feminism with a double coupon. You want the privileges of equality and the benefits of chivalry at the same time. You want the freedom to do you, while a man waits patiently in the wings, ready to bankroll your glow-up and tolerate your emotional chaos. That is not empowerment. That is emotional socialism.

Men see this clearly. They watch the pattern. They witness selfishness dressed up as confidence, the attitude disguised as standards, and the arrogance mislabeled as independence. No man will sign up for a one-sided deal where you take endlessly while contributing nothing of value.

Real empowerment does not demand a pedestal. Real empowerment earns one. Women who understand this still win. Women who do not will keep wondering why men stopped playing along.

Your Personality Flaws

• • •

If behavior is what men notice first, personality is what makes them stay or walk away. A man can overlook a bad date, but he cannot overlook a bad personality. Marriage is not built on looks, money, or witty captions. It is built on character. And when a woman carries entitlement, arrogance, hostility, or emotional immaturity, no man will sign his life to that.

Personality shows up in the trivial things. It is how she talks to waiters, how she treats her friends, and how she behaves when life does not go her way. Men watch these moments closely because they know they will be living with that personality every single day. A beautiful face can catch his eye, but a toxic personality will push him out the door.

Modern culture tells women that personality does not matter and that men should love them unconditionally, no matter how they treat people. Men know better. They understand that a bad personality turns into constant conflict, cold silences, resentment, and emotional warfare that no wedding ring can fix. Men are not searching for perfection. They seek peace, loyalty, stability, and a partner who makes life easier rather than heavier.

This section exposes the personality flaws that make marriage unappealing for men. These are not harmless quirks or cute imperfections. They are serious warnings that tell a man he will be sacrificing his happiness for someone who does not value him. A woman with the wrong personality may get a date, but she will never get a husband. No man will choose to spend his life tied to misery wearing high heels.

Truth #8 – Grow Up, Princess!!!

Princess Thinking

You grew up on movies where the princess waits while Prince Charming does all the work. In your mind, the plan has not changed. You imagine a man showing up, proving himself worthy, showering you with devotion, placing you in a castle, and funding your dream life while you contribute nothing but your presence.

You are not a princess. You are a regular person like everyone else. You do not deserve what you have not earned, and you do not deserve more than a man can realistically provide. You are not getting a prince, and you are not living in a castle with a bunch of peasants doing everything for you.

The harshest truth is straightforward. Even if a man were a prince and you lived in a castle while he showered you with diamonds, it still would not be enough. Just like Eve, you would still want more because the problem is not your circumstances. The problem is your mindset, and entitlement always outgrows reality.

Princess thinking does not end with a crown. It ends with resentment, disappointment, and a lifetime of blaming men for failing to satisfy a ridiculous fantasy.

You Don't Understand Men

How do you expect a man to marry you when you believe his primary job is to make you happy? Why would a man sign up for that when your mood can shift faster than a weather app? You could marry him on Monday and be searching for divorce lawyers by Friday. The problem is simple. You do not understand men.

A man's purpose is not to be your emotional butler. He is not your therapist, your comfort animal, or your crisis manager. His role is to lead the family with protection, and handling responsibility. For generations, women respected that. They knew masculinity was the backbone of the family. Now, many roll their eyes at those same qualities while still expecting him to kill spiders, fix leaks, lift heavy things, and absorb emotional meltdowns like a monk in training.

You want leadership but refuse to respect the leader. You desire strength but mock masculinity. You crave tenderness but lose attraction the moment he expresses vulnerability. You seek a partnership but treat him like a handyman with feelings. No man can win when the rules keep changing.

You want a man, but only if he acts like your best girlfriend. That contradiction is why men walk away. They understand marriage has become an audition for the impossible. Be strong but soft, confident but gentle, dominant but compliant, masculine but emotional, stoic but expressive, assertive but careful. No man can juggle all of that without losing himself.

The truth is painfully simple. You do not want to understand men. You want to rewrite them. But no man will volunteer to be a rough draft for your personality project. A man would rather walk alone than lose himself trying to fit your fantasy.

You Blame Everyone But You

Women reinforce their own bad behaviors while insisting that men are wrong for noticing them.

Men are not looking to marry a woman who refuses to take accountability. We're used to that... and all of the jokes and memes aside, it drives us insane. Many women blame everything except themselves for the state of their relationships. You tell yourself men are intimidated, that the universe is sending signs. You convince yourself you are unlucky or misunderstood.

Here is the truth. You are single because you avoid accountability. You make poor choices, chase the wrong men, ignore red flags, and refuse to acknowledge your part in the chaos. When everything falls apart, you point at him, the dating pool, society, your ex, your trauma, or anything else nearby. Never at yourself.

You want a high-value man while offering no introspection. You want loyalty without growth, respect without humility. You want love without responsibility, and you will not fix what you refuse to admit exists.

And that is the biggest turn-off of all. Nothing is ever your fault. Every relationship fails because he was not ready, not mature enough, not emotionally available, or not aligned with your healing journey. If you cheat, you claim he made you feel neglected. If you lash out, you say you were triggered. If you sabotage, you call it protecting your peace.

Men do not want to play therapist to someone allergic to accountability. You treat criticism as abuse and treat advice as an attack. But a real woman owns her flaws. She does not spin every disaster into a victim story to protect her ego.

If your first instinct is to blame, deflect, rewrite the narrative, and shield your pride at all costs, do not act surprised when men protect their peace by walking away from you.

Truth #9 – Main Characters & Fairy Tales

Main Character Syndromes

You strut around like you have theme music playing overhead. Every minor inconvenience becomes a personal attack. Every disagreement becomes a dramatic plot twist. You have convinced yourself that life is your movie, and everyone else is background noise whose only job is to support your storyline.

But men are not lining up to play your supporting actor in a never-ending rom-com where you cry because Target ran out of oat milk and expect applause for blocking your mother as "self-care." Real men do not want to be props in your self-absorbed production. They are not auditioning to be your emotional lighting crew or your emotional stuntmen. They are tired of living in the shadows of a movie that only exists in your head.

If you insist on always being the main character, what role does the man get? Supporting cast? Comic relief? Background filler who exists only to enhance your angles? No self-respecting man will sign up to be an extra in your woman fantasy film. Men do not marry scripts, and they do not marry fantasies. They are not signing contracts to act in the fairy-tale version of your life.

Fairy Tale Thinking Will Fail You

Modern women love to claim they want a traditional man. The protector. The provider. The rock. But you are not a traditional woman. You want him to carry the weight of tradition while you enjoy all the freedoms and perks of modern independence. That is not balance. That is delusion.

Traditional men once needed traditional women. That world is gone. Modern men can cook, clean, pay their own bills, and live without chaos. They are checking out, ghosting, opting out, or avoiding commitment entirely. Not because they hate women, but because they see the deal clearly. Men are expected to be old-school providers, while women choose which parts of tradition still feel empowering and discard the rest.

One man summarized it perfectly:
"You want the benefits of being a modern woman, but you want men to move in a traditional way. You want men to spend money on you, but you refuse to spend yours, even when you make as much as they do."

That is not a partnership. That is hypocrisy. Women hate hearing this part, but the fairy tale is not failing men. It is failing you. The longer you cling to this double standard, the fewer men will even bother stepping into the role you think you deserve.

Truth #10 – Boys See Their Mothers (Childhood Impressions)

When you wonder why men hesitate to marry, remember this. Every man was once a boy. Boys notice more than you think. They saw every eye roll, every insult, every bitter comment whispered under your breath. They heard every time you called a man weak, lazy, or useless. You thought you were venting. But boys understood the message clearly. And no man forgets what he learned about women from the woman who raised him.

It was often a woman who attacked the image of his father, then turned around and expected her son to become the kind of man she would respect. You tore down his first role model and then wondered why he refuses to step into the same position. You cannot raise a king while destroying the man who taught him what it means to be a man. So now he is grown, and he remembers. He watched what modern women did to his father, his uncle, and his brothers, and he refuses to line up for the same punishment.

He is determined NOT to suffer a similar fate.

And one of the clearest things they learned was this. Your real weapon was not logic or love. It was guilt. Guilt became the invisible contract he never signed but always paid. Guilt is how you turned his needs into selfishness. It is how you converted his happiness into a crime. It is how you made freedom feel like disrespect.

It never begins loudly. It always starts subtly. With comments such as, "Why did you not call me back?" or "You are going out again?!" A man will answer those questions, thinking he is being considerate. He is wrong. He is being conditioned; trained to place your emotions above his own needs. Women train men to feel guilty for pursuing their happiness. This conditioning comes in three phases:

1. **Emotional framing**
   - Not real questions, but accusations disguised as concern.
   - "Don't worry about me. I'll be fine."
   - He is suddenly on trial for wanting normal things.
2. **Silent sabotage**
   - The cold shoulder. The strategic sighs. The sad, hollow expression that makes him apologize for things he did not do.
3. **Currency**
   - Eventually, you will not need words. A single look becomes currency. Like Pavlov's dog, he changes his behavior before you even speak.

Yes. This is "The Curse of Eve" again.

People regularly ask, "Why did Adam listen to Eve and eat from the Tree of Knowledge?" Was he just naive? Was he a weak man? Well, maybe he was... But men in love try to keep their women satisfied and at peace. Everyone knows a man who has made a bad decision due to a woman.

Over a long period of time, a man's individuality disappears. Not because a woman destroyed him directly, but because guilt taught him to erase or quiet his urges and true nature.

And here is the part women never consider. Boys saw this happen to the men they respect, long before they became men. They watched their fathers shrink and watched his guilt become a leash. They watched men lose themselves under the weight of emotional pressure. They saw their fathers reduced to obligation, stripped of joy, and crushed by expectations they could never meet.

These boys have now grown into men. They are not bitter, angry, or hateful. They are simply choosing to walk away before the erosion happens to them.

They learned the lessons early, and they are not willing to live the same story.

Truth #11 – Women Bring Chaos

There are four marks of chaos: disorder, lack of control, unpredictability, and instability. Sound familiar? For many men, these issues are not abstract concepts. They are daily experiences. Most arguments can be traced back to one of these four: overspending, reckless decisions, emotional spirals, or creating problems out of nothing. The women worth marrying reduce chaos and replace it with "peace", while the rest embody it.

Men do not hate women. They hate the storm that often comes with them. You stir drama into situations that were peaceful, and bring emotion where logic is needed. Moments of calm can escalate into conflict because of you. A casual conversation can become an argument, and you can switch from flirty to furious in a flash, calling it passion.

. You inject feelings into every decision and then act shocked when men need space. That is not passion. That is turbulence. And men are tired of paying the emotional bill for it.

Even the trivial things expose a deeper pattern. When you park your car crooked and over the line, you think it is nothing. He does not just see bad parking. He sees disorganization, carelessness, and a preview of larger problems ahead. While you think it is trivial, he thinks, "If she cannot park her car straight, how can she handle a real crisis?" What you call a cute, quirky personality, is what he calls mental instability.

Men do not crave chaos. They crave order, rhythm, and peace.

One minute everything is fine, and the next minute, you are crashing out because he liked a social media photo of a girl he grew up with from 2009. Your mood swings have mood swings. Somehow, he always ends up cast as the villain in the story you wrote in your own head. Peace becomes impossible when every silence becomes suspicion and every small decision becomes drama.

The opposite of chaos is peace. But your version of peace requires him to agree with everything you say, apologize for things he never did, and read your mind like a psychic on salary. That is not peace. That is submission through exhaustion. Men do not want a lifetime of walking on eggshells. They do not want their home to feel like a storm shelter. They want calm, safety, and stability.

That is why men hesitate. Freedom may be lonely, but at least it is quiet.

Chaos wears men down. A man can only juggle so much drama before he starts wondering whether any relationship is worth the emotional storm that comes with it. And just when he thinks he has reached his limit, biology enters the conversation. Women may downplay it, but men notice. They notice how many partners you have had. They notice whether you take care of your body. Men do not see these things as shallow. They see them as necessary for their financial and emotional survival.

A man who has already battled through noise, conflict, and instability is not signing up for extra baggage or neglect. Which brings us to the next truth. The cold math of body count and fitness.

Why Men Won't Marry You

Fitness and Body Counts

• • •

When it comes to marriage, men notice two things immediately: how a woman takes care of herself, and how many men have already had "access" to her. These are not shallow observations. They are indicators of discipline, values, and long-term potential. Women are told by society, and feminists, that these things should not matter, but every honest man knows they do. Fitness and body count are not just numbers. They are signals. And men read those signals clearly.

A woman's fitness shows effort. It shows she has self-control, respect for her health, and pride in her body. Men know attraction dies quickly when discipline is missing. No man wants to build a future with someone who has already given up on herself. Fitness is not about looking like a model. It is about demonstrating the strength and consistency needed to care for yourself and one day, a family.

Body count reveals a different truth. It tells him whether you guard intimacy or treat it casually. Men care about this because they want to feel valued, not like they are just the next name in a long lineup. A high body count may be rebranded as liberation, but men see it as instability and risk. No man wants to commit his life, resources, and legacy to someone who has been careless with hers.

Modern culture tries to shame men for caring about these things. It tells them they are insecure, controlling, or judgmental. Reality says otherwise. Men do not risk their futures for a woman who shows no discipline or loyalty. They may spend a night with her, but they will not spend a lifetime with her.

This section explains why fitness and body count matter far more than women want to admit. It exposes why these two factors are deal-breakers for serious men and why ignoring them is the fastest way to disqualify yourself from ever being chosen.

Truth #12 – Body Count & Fitness Matter

Men care about your body count. They always have, and they always will. You have been told it should not matter, that your past is private, and that men who care are insecure. Nice story, but completely false. Men do not want to commit their lives, money, peace, or loyalty to someone who has treated intimacy like a revolving door. That is not being free. Men see it clearly as baggage.

You say, "Do not judge me by my past," but men are not judging your past. They are judging your patterns. A high body count does not say empowered. It says impulsive, unstable, reckless, and emotionally detached. It tells him you lack restraint, that intimacy means little to you, and that loyalty may be a temporary concept. It tells him that if you did not protect your own body, you are unlikely to protect his legacy.

Live however you want. No one is stopping you. Just do not act surprised when men are not lining up to marry you after you have toured the zip codes. The men you want are searching for something rare, not something repeatedly sampled. Rarity is created through discipline, not through access.

And yes, there is a double standard. Men can get away with more. Why? Because biology itself is a double standard. One bull can impregnate an entire field of cows. One stallion can breed an entire herd. One male lion mates with an entire pride of lionesses. Nature does not care about your modern slogans. Men are wired to spread seed. Women are wired to choose selectively. You do not get to rewrite evolutionary law because an influencer convinced you otherwise.

Men want to feel like they have something special, not something community issued. Your sexual experience does not make you wife material. It makes you less desirable to the kind of men who actually have options and may want a wife. A man who has built himself, wants a woman who values intimacy, not someone who treats it like a hobby or a sport.

So yes, body count mattered before social media. It matters now, and it will matter long after the trends fade. Do you really believe that a man dreams of walking down the aisle with community property wearing a dress? No, he dreams of choosing a woman who has the discipline to value what she claims to cherish.

You're Not Fit

Women demand men who are fit in every category. Financially secure. Emotionally stable. Physically strong. Disciplined. Motivated. Responsible. But here is the question you do not want to face. Are you fit for marriage?

If you are overweight, drowning in debt, ruled by emotions, and bouncing from crisis to crisis, you are not a partner. You are a liability with lip gloss. Marriage is not something you deserve automatically. It is something you qualify for. You cannot bring chaos instead of consistency, complaints instead of contribution, and instability instead of support, then expect a man to commit his future to you.

If you cannot commit to a gym schedule, a budget, or emotional self-control, do not expect a man to commit. Men do not want to repair projects. They want partners who already come with stability.

And men notice when a woman marries in shape, and then stops caring. That is their nightmare. They invest early, only to watch their wife quit the moment she gets the ring. Treat your body like you treat a job interview. You would not fake your qualifications and expect to stay employed once the truth comes out. Marriage works the same way. If you are not fit for the role, you will not be chosen.

We will now move on to makeup. The layers of foundation, the contouring, the industrial-strength lashes, the filters, the ring lights, the FaceApp edits. That is not enhancement. That is deception. Men see it. You say you do it for yourself, but your camera roll tells the real story. It is a performance for attention, validation, and competition.

And here is the hardest truth. You are not as attractive as you think you are. The filters, the angles, the push-up bras, the lighting, the edits, and the simps in your DMs have inflated your ego but not your value. Men are visual creatures. They always have been. The men who most women want; the tall, dark, and handsome—are rare. And unicorns, the rarest of them all, do not settle for 5s and 6s out of 10. They choose 9s and 10s because they can.

When you remove the app filters, turn off the ring light, and wipe off the makeup mask, you should remember not to overestimate your Sexual Marketplace Value (SMV). This SMV is what men place upon you. Men rate you more naturally because the truth is simple. Men do not marry potential or online illusions. You do not get to assign yourself an SMV.

Men want to marry someone fit, feminine, and real. If you are not bringing those qualities, you are not contributing anything worth committing to.

Truth #13 – You Think You Are "The Table"

Women love to say, "I am the table," as if it is a mic-drop moment that ends the conversation. But if you were truly the table, you would bring stability, support, and value, not attitude, demands, and an extensive list of tasks you refuse to do. Saying you are the table means nothing when all you have to offer is entitlement, opinions, and reheated trauma. A man does not want a table with trust issues and a social media addiction. He wants a partner who makes life better, not harder.

Here is the truth. Men build the table. They create structure, protection, provision, and peace. They bring the foundation of stability. You bring eyelashes, expectations, and a sense of entitlement. That is not contribution. That is decoration. And when a man asks what you offer, instead of answering, you get offended, change the subject, or accuse him of being insecure. Then you wonder why he walks away and chooses someone else.

Your presence is not a prize. Your attention is not a gift. Men are not searching for a table. They are searching for a wife. Someone who knows how to sit at the table with gratitude, bring something worth sharing, and protect the bond she claims to want. That is partnership and what keeps a man committed.

Declaring yourself to be the table might sound powerful on Instagram, but in real life it makes men laugh. A table is an object where you put things, not something you build a life with. Once men see through that illusion, they start to wonder what else about you is based on slogans instead of substance.

And this is where your choices catch up to you. The men you rejected. The men you entertained. The chaos you preferred. The good men you overlooked for the bad ones who wasted your time. Men notice. They see the history, the patterns, and the priorities. When they realize you keep choosing drama over peace and attention over stability, they stop offering you a seat altogether.

Men are not blind. We see who you really are behind the slogans. And when the illusion fades, so does our interest. Be real. Banish any suggestion that you "Are the Table" from your life immediately. No man wants to marry any woman who says such a silly statement.

Kelly Ruff

Cultural and Societal Influences

• • •

Men do not make decisions about marriage in isolation. Every choice they consider is shaped by the culture they live in and the pressures society puts on them. And right now, the culture is loud, hostile, and stacked against them. From social media to television to the courtroom, the message is simple: men are disposable, women are victims, and marriage is another tool for securing money, power, or sympathy. With those odds, why would any man walk willingly into the fire?

Modern culture tells women they can have everything without giving anything in return. It encourages them to chase the top 10% of men, treat average men as invisible, and then complain when no one wants to commit. It celebrates selfishness and excuses chaos. Society backs it up with laws and double standards that punish men for being men and reward women for failure.

The result is a dating market where men feel like targets, not partners.

These influences are not background noise. They are the daily reality men face. They watch women brag about not needing a man while still expecting men to pay for every date and every convenience. They see divorce celebrated as empowerment. They perceive broken homes as new beginnings. They view loyalty mocked and dysfunction praised. They witness men ridiculed for caring and shamed for setting boundaries.

Men understand what it means to marry into this culture. It means stepping into a role where they will be judged harshly, blamed frequently, and valued conditionally. It means being cast as the villain in a story that was written long before they arrived.

This section reveals how cultural and societal forces have poisoned the well of modern relationships. It shows how outside influences promote entitlement, weaken accountability, and encourage women to behave in ways that push men away. Men are not rejecting marriage because they hate women. They are rejecting it because the culture applauds everything that destroys it.

Truth #14 – You Chose the Bear (Mistrust of Men)

There was a viral post asking single women a simple question: Who would you rather be stuck with in the woods, a strange man, or a bear? And the overwhelming answer from modern women was the bear. A real bear. A creature built to rip, crush, and shred anything in its path. An animal that kills without hesitation and sometimes starts eating before the prey is even dead. That is who women said they trusted more than an ordinary man who might build a fire, find water, and keep them alive. The idea is so offensive to rational men.

Let us be clear. Bears are not cute. They are not cuddly. They are not misunderstood woodland pets. They are apex predators. The fact that women confidently chose a wild animal over an average man tells men everything they need to know about the modern mindset. In your eyes, the average man is more dangerous than a creature designed by nature to maul people. That is the level of distrust men now face, simply for existing.

You claim you are strong and independent, yet you panic when a man holds the door. You claim you want protection, yet you openly admit you trust a grizzly more than a decent guy standing next to you. You cannot have it both ways. If the average man is truly more frightening than a 600-pound carnivore, then the problem is not the man. The problem is your perception.

If that is really your choice, then fine. No man can argue with what you prefer. But do not be shocked when men stop volunteering themselves for marriage. If you would rather pick a predator in the woods, then men are smart enough to let you wander into those woods alone.

Your choices tell the story. Every time you ignore a good man for a bad one, it reveals what you actually value. Every time you chase the dangerous option, the chaotic option, or the high-status option that will never commit, men take notes. And once men recognize the pattern, they realize it is not about one troubled relationship. It is about a consistent preference for the wrong men.

That pattern has a name: the **Pareto Principle**, the obsession with the top percentage of men. It is the allure of **hypergamy**, pushing women to chase the **"Evil Sixes"**: six feet tall, six figure income, and six-pack abs. It is the fantasy of securing the top man while still expecting average men to wait patiently in the background as a backup. This is not a single poor decision. It reflects an entire dating economy molded by unrealistic expectations.

Modern men see this clearly. They are aware that many women do not fear men; women fear accountability. The mere suggestion that you'd rather be in the woods with a bear shows a severe allergy to reality. An argument can be made that any woman who would suggest she'd rather be in the woods with a bear over a man has a mental issue. Such a woman may, in fact, be acknowledging that she would rather die than accept the idea that she might be dependent on a man for her survival.

When smart, reasonable men see that you've said you would choose a bear before you choose them, they already know that you would never be their wife.

Truth #15 – The Pareto Principle, the Evil 666, and Hypergamy

You may have heard about the **Pareto Principle** if you've taken a business class in the last 40 years. *Vilfredo Pareto* was an Italian Economist who observed that 80% of Italian Land was owned by 20% of the population. Through his study, he observed that this "80/20 Rule" could be applied to many circumstances, from gardening to warfare, and of course, to business.

Yes, the Pareto Principle applies to dating and relationships as well. As an example, 80% of women are chasing the top 20% of men. The tall, wealthy, confident man women think they deserve. Women throw themselves at these men all the time, not realizing that he has no incentive to commit. Why would that 20% man settle down when he has a constant rotation of attention, validation, and bedroom options?

Meanwhile, the other 80% of men, the loyal ones with stable lives and steady hearts, are ignored. These are the men who would actually build something with you, but you call them boring, too short, or not ambitious enough. They are the very men who would give you the life you say you want, but your standards will not allow you to see them. You are average yet convinced that your 500 social media followers elevated you into royalty.

Here is the difference between men and women. Yes, men also admire the top 20% of women, but men are realistic. If they cannot attract those women, they adjust. They pick a good woman and build with her. That is why men do not talk about "manifesting" or "finding their person." Men live in reality, not fantasy.

The 6-6-6 Fantasy

Then there is the famous 6-6-6 checklist: six feet tall, six-pack abs, and six figures. Many modern women consider this the bare minimum. That is not a standard. That is a hallucination. Here is the math you refuse to do:

- Around 14% of US men are six feet or taller.
- Roughly 9 to 10% of men earn more than $100,000 per year.
- About 8% of men have visible abs.

A man with all three is less than 1% of the male population. And that fraction of 1% includes every race, every age group, every sexual orientation, every married man, and every man who wants nothing to do with you! In simple English,

The man you want barely exists!

Additionally, The men who meet these standards know they are rare and are in high demand. They have options—endless options.

Why would a man with status, money, and options settle for a woman who brings attitude, debt, a history of poor decisions, or a list of men she already slept with? The women these men choose tend to be younger, kinder, fitter, and far more pleasant.

And when your 6-6-6 fantasy collapses, the only thing left is six cats, six years without a date, and six figures in debt. That is not empowerment. That is lifestyle delusion.

Here is another truth you are avoiding: you are not just chasing wealth or physical attractiveness. You are chasing pretty men. You scroll past responsible men because their hairline retired early, but you fight over the Calvin Klein wannabe in the tank top. Meanwhile, you expect men to ignore your attitude, your children, your financial mess, and your lack of discipline.

A man can overlook flaws, but he will not overlook arrogance. The higher your demands, the more obvious your shortcomings become.

The men you want are the same men every woman wants. In other words, those men get to choose. Most women do not qualify, which is the part you refuse to see. The higher your fantasy climbs, the smaller your window becomes, and the faster reality catches up to you.

Hypergamy

Hypergamy is the drive to form a relationship with someone of higher status. It is the subconscious desire for a man who is taller, richer, stronger, smarter, and more successful than you. This is why women chase power. It is why women break up with stable boyfriends for men they do not even love, simply because the new man has a flashier car or a better title. And when the gamble backfires, many try to crawl back to the man they once called boring, hoping he forgot the insult.

Look at dating apps. Women swipe past hundreds of men they label as ugly, boring, or not good enough, all chasing the same elite few. The best option is the same for everyone, which means those men hold all the power. They choose, and they rarely choose women who treat them as prizes to be worshipped.

That is hypergamy in motion. Women chase upward. Men pick realistically. The men at the top decide, and they rarely choose women who act entitled to them.

The Pattern

Your choices reveal the truth. Every time you picked the wrong man, it showed what you actually valued. Once men see the pattern, they stop feeling sorry for you. They know this is not a single mistake. It is the Pareto Principle at work, the fantasy of the 6-6-6 man, and the biological pull of hypergamy. It is the entire dating economy pushing you toward the top while ignoring the good men who would have chosen you.

This is not just a math and dating problem. It is the entire structure of modern relationships working against you.

The Pareto Principle in Action

- 20% of single men sleep with 80% of single women.
- 80% of single moms date only 20% of single dads.
- 80% of women desire only 20% of attractive men.
- 20% of traits men value, account for 80% of their relationship satisfaction.
- 80% of divorces are filed by women, 20% by men.
- 20% of female beliefs cause 80% of men's hesitation to marry them.

*** *These are +/- values, NOT exact*

Truth #16 – Biology Rules You

Men understand something women pretend not to know. Women are ruled by biology. Instincts drive choices more than slogans, hashtags, or empowerment speeches ever will. Women lie to secure commitment, cheat to hedge their bets, and sometimes cross moral lines with a friend's boyfriend or another woman's husband if they believe it gives them a better chance at survival. This is not romance. It is instinct in heels.

History shows the pattern. During World War II, Germany invaded and occupied France. Many French believed Germany would win the war. How did they respond? Well, countless French women switched sides overnight. They dated Nazis and other German soldiers while French men were still fighting and dying for their country.  It's harsh, but real! Women run to power, protection, and stability. This is not cruelty. It is biology making decisions long before feelings ever show up.

Humans love to pretend we are above nature. We are not. We build skyscrapers and record TikToks, but we operate the same way every other animal does. Across the animal kingdom, females seek safety and provision, while males compete for access to females. That is the evolutionary bargain. It has not changed. It will not change just because someone updated their pronouns or listened to a relationship podcast.

People insist that humans are "different," but nature does not care about those claims. A mosquito can kill a human. A cow can crush one. A virus can humble entire nations. For all our pride, we are still animals following the same primal script. The only difference is that now we scroll through those instincts on a phone.

Biology does not care about your opinions. Nature does not recognize your feelings. It does not negotiate with your preferences. Women select for strength, security, confidence, and competence, and men pursue youth, loyalty, and femininity. These instincts have been around for thousands of years and will continue to exist long after our modern cultures burn out.

Biology sets the stage, but culture writes the rules. For centuries, the rules were simple. Men worked, built, and protected. Women nurtured, supported, and created stability at home. It was not perfect, but it worked because both sides knew their roles. Then the contract was torn up. Women demanded the benefits without the duties, the rewards without the responsibilities, and the power without the sacrifice. Men paid attention.

When the rules changed, men changed too. They stopped volunteering for a game where they could only lose. They stopped pretending biology did not matter. Because the truth is simple, you can disguise instincts with trends, therapy quotes, and modern slogans, but underneath it all, you are still ruled by the same primal forces that shaped humanity since the beginning.

You are not above nature. You are simply another animal, but one with a smartphone.

Truth #17 – Women Broke the Contract

Men do not want to marry you because women have broken the contract. For thousands of years, the deal between men and women was simple and understood without debate. Men had their roles and worked themselves into the ground for their families. They created safety, stability, and structure. In return, women nurtured, supported, respected their man, and served as his help mate in life. The bible refers to a "helper" (Genesis 2:18). The arrangement worked so well that it built legacies, formed families, and stabilized entire societies.

Then something changed. Modern women tore that contract to pieces. Instead of loyalty, men now find half-naked selfies of their girlfriends, and sometimes their wives, online. Instead of partnership, men get divorce threats, conditional love, and endless speeches about independence delivered from houses they paid for. Women did not just break the contract. They shredded it, set it on fire, and posted the ashes with a caption about empowerment. And now they wonder why men are not lining up to sign a new agreement.

The irony is painful. Women still want all the traditional benefits of marriage. They want his income, his protection, his leadership, his problem-solving ability, and his sacrifice. What they do not want, is to offer anything traditional in return. Being a helpmate is beneath them, but his paycheck is not. Cooking is oppression but expecting him to pay every bill is empowerment. Respecting the man they chose is outdated, but demanding he exceed every expectation is now considered a right.

Men noticed the shift. They watched loyalty change into online attention-seeking. They watched respect turn into attitude. They watched as sacrifice was replaced by slogans. They watched marriage become a one-sided arrangement where men give everything and receive extraordinarily little in return. And they adjusted.

Here is what the contract used to be, and what it became:

Old Contract (Prehistoric–1998)	Modern Contract (1999–Present)
Men protect and provide	Men protect and provide
Women nurture and support	Women demand support but reject nurturing
Women bring partnership and sacrifice	Women bring entitlement and attitude
Women show loyalty to the family	Women seek validation from strangers online
Women share responsibility	Women have one-sided expectations
Divorce was rare and stigmatized, with the wife leaving with nothing.	Divorce is common and the wife gets the house, alimony, and the kids.

Men read the fine print. They realized they were being asked to work harder, pay more, sacrifice more, and risk more while receiving less of what men have always valued. They watched as courts rewarded women who left and punished men who stayed. They watched marriage turn into a gamble with terrible odds. A gamble where men lose their money, their children, their homes, and sometimes their mental health. They started asking the obvious question: Why sign up for this?

You cannot have it both ways. You cannot mock masculinity while expecting men to provide. You cannot reject tradition while demanding traditional benefits. You cannot insult men for being men and then expect those same men to risk everything for you. That is not equality. That is entitlement disguised as progress.

Modern women replaced loyalty with delusion. They replaced partnership with demands. They replaced humility with arrogance. And men adjusted accordingly. Few men are foolish enough to sign that contract twice. Many are not willing to sign it even once.

And when the old social contract between men and women died, something else took its place. Social media became the new rulebook. Validation now comes from "likes", "thirsty comments", and strangers in DMs. Women scream that they do not need men, then spend hours editing photos to get attention from men they will never meet.

Men see the contradiction. They see that the phone has already replaced the approach, the chase, and the pursuit. They now see how replaceable the entire dating game has become.

Men are not rejecting marriage because they hate women. They are rejecting marriage because women destroyed the contract that once made marriage worth it.

Truth #18 – Social Media, No Approaches & "I Don't Need No Man"

Social media has replaced relationships. Your phone is your lover, your therapist, your diary, and your stage. Instagram knows more about your mood than your man does. You broadcast everything: brunch photos, breakdowns, arguments, and passive-aggressive quotes about "how useless men are." You treat your relationship like content, then wonder why no man wants to build something real with you. No man wants his private life turned into a soap opera for four hundred strangers and three exes every time he forgets to call.

Social media has turned you into a performance artist. Everything is curated, staged, and filtered for attention. You do not solve problems; you post about them. You do not fix your relationship; you subtweet it. You are more loyal to the validation of strangers than to the man in your life, and men see it. They witness the addiction, the dependence, and the craving for attention. Competing with a phone is a losing game, and men are done trying.

No man wants to be a prop in your highlight reel. No man wants to date a woman who lives online. If your validation lives on a screen, your relationships will stay there too: shallow, temporary, and one swipe away from collapse. Men do not want to be your content. They want to be your partner. And if you cannot put the phone down for him, he will put you down as a distant option.

Men Will Not Approach You

Women complain that men no longer approach but let us be honest. You turned the simple act of saying hello into a public trial. Men are not afraid of rejection. They are afraid of being filmed, mocked, canceled, or accused of harassment for attempting basic human interaction. You told men not to catcall, not to flirt at the gym, not to talk to you at the store unless they looked like a movie star, and only if you were in the mood. You trained men to see you as a liability, not an opportunity.

Now, women are lonely, swiping endlessly, confused about where the good men went. Here is where they are: minding their own business, speaking to no one, and avoiding risk the same way they avoid lawsuits. Men have learned that one misunderstood moment can cost them their reputation, their job, or their freedom. When the price of hello is humiliation, silence becomes the safest option.

You built the wall and made yourself unapproachable. You added alarms, guard dogs, and camera phones. Do not cry when no man wants to climb it. Respect goes both ways, and if men no longer feel safe offering it, they will not offer their presence either.

You Say, You "Don't Need No Man"

You made your declaration loud and clear. You posted it, repeated it, lived by it, and built your personality around it. You claimed independence, bragged about self-sufficiency, and called men unnecessary. You spent a decade chanting about boss energy and emotional autonomy. Men paid attention. They believed you.

Now that men have stepped back, you are wondering where the good ones went. They went where they were wanted. They moved on from the women who treated them as optional accessories, only useful when it was time to pay, fix something, or absorb an emotional meltdown.

After years of telling men they are replaceable, you cannot expect them to line up when you finally decide you are ready for commitment at thirty-five. Men heard you the first time.

Feminism did not help you. It finished you. It taught you that acting like a man would make you valuable, when the reality is that masculine men do not want masculine partners. They want feminine, warm, stable women. No man dreams of marrying his own reflection.

You doubled down on independence and then wondered why the men you desire lost interest. You were not empowered. You were repelling the very men you hoped to attract. And when you did find a decent man, you ran straight to the Sisterhood for advice. That infamous circle encouraged you to break up over inconveniences, red flags they invented, and expectations they themselves cannot meet.

Instead of asking men what they value, you asked your friend with three baby daddies, a part-time boyfriend, and a burner Instagram account if you should leave a man for not buying you a $300 steak. And of course she said, "Girl, you deserve better."

The Sisterhood is a cult. It chants that all men are trash, while its members cry when no men ask them out, open doors for them, or spend a single dollar on them. You cared more about the approval of women who do not live with you, sleep with you, or build with you than the approval of the man who actually tried.

Men have stopped playing that game. No man will marry a woman who loudly declares she does not need men, or worse, behaves like a man herself.

When enough filters, slogans, and empowerment memes fail to produce the relationship you want, the truth finally appears. Under all the noise, women still want happiness. But happiness costs something. It requires sacrifice, compromise, and putting someone else before yourself. Modern women preach self-love but forget that relationships run on selflessness. Men see the contradiction. You want the reward without the responsibility, and that is why the self-respecting men you desire and want will continue to walk away.

Truth #19 – You Want "Happiness" but Won't Sacrifice Anything for It.

Women today treat happiness like it is sacred. Marriage, family, commitment, stability—none of it stands a chance against a change in mood. One rough patch, one argument, one unmet expectation, and you are suddenly downloading divorce papers like it is a wellness ritual. Women have been indoctrinated to believe that their personal happiness is more important than vows, unity, or the well-being of everyone around them. Marriage is not a commitment to you. It is a subscription. When the feelings fade, you cancel the plan.

Men do not operate that way and will stay miserable if it means keeping the family together. They sacrifice happiness to uphold duty, responsibility, and structure. While women sacrifice duty in pursuit of happiness, men grind through the storms because they see the bigger picture. Women chase emotional highs without considering the wreckage those choices create.

Do not act confused when men hesitate to commit. They have watched too many women treat marriage like a mood ring. When the color changes, the vows disappear. That is not love. That is emotional narcissism masquerading as "finding yourself." Men see the pattern clearly and are stepping back before they are blindsided by another, "I am not happy anymore" proclamation.

Women Do Not Understand Sacrifice

Everything meaningful in life requires sacrifice, and a man will not marry you because you do not understand this basic truth. For example, to earn money, you sacrifice time and energy. To gain education, you forgo comfort and rest. When it comes to marriage, you are supposed to sacrifice selfishness, pride, and convenience. But the average modern woman believes she should sacrifice nothing.

Men know better and expect sacrifice. They take difficult jobs, lose sleep, break their bodies, and grind every day to keep the lights on and the household running. They do this without applause, without praise, and often without anyone noticing. Sacrifice is built into manhood.

Women, on the other hand, sacrifice only when it feels good or when there is an audience to witness it. The moment something stops serving your happiness, you leave. You do not stay in the trenches with your man. You walk out the second the relationship requires effort. Then you insult him for wanting to relax after carrying the weight of the world all day. You treat giving up bottomless brunch like it is a war story.

Men suffer silently for their families. Women post selfies about "self-love" when they skip a girls' trip. That is why men are walking away. The truth is simple: men sacrifice by default. Women sacrifice only when demanded.

And when sacrifice disappears, convenience takes over. Nothing is more convenient than an app. Dating apps have rewired modern thinking. Every face becomes a swipe, every connection becomes a transaction, and every relationship feels disposable. It is the mindset that turns people into options instead of partners. When women treat relationships like fast food, always replacing instead of repairing, men stop believing marriage is worth the risk.

Relationships cannot survive convenience. Marriage cannot survive entitlement. And happiness without sacrifice is not happiness at all. It is a fantasy, one that men are no longer willing to fund.

Truth #20 – You Have "App Brain"

Dating applications (apps) for your phone have rewritten your entire understanding of men. You have spent years on phone software, swiping left and right, judging men like a casting director for a reality show. If he is not pretty enough, tall enough, or filtered enough, you swipe left in half a second... and go to the next.

Every other woman is doing the same thing. You are all chasing the same 20% of men, the ones who are tall, fit, handsome, and wealthy. But those men do not need you. They have more options than they can handle. While you are treating them like prizes, they are treating you like backups.

Your "App Brain" has trained you to believe that normal men do not exist. The stable, loyal, hardworking men who would build a family with you become invisible because they are not "app attractive." Meanwhile, the flashy ones who match your fantasy, are matching with dozens of women every day. You are not standing out. You are standing in line.

'And it gets worse. App Brain becomes an addiction. Women stay on dating apps even when they have a boyfriend, and sometimes even when they have a husband. You scroll, swipe, and "just look" for attention. You call it harmless. Men call it disrespect. You are not chasing men. You are chasing validation from strangers. And men see it.

App Brain also destroys your self-image. You start believing you are a "10" because you are getting swipes and Direct Messages (DMs). But attention is not valuable. Men swipe on everything. They cast a wide net because they are generally looking for fun instead of relationships. Women swipe on one type, usually the top-tier men. So those fire emojis in your inbox do not mean you are special. They mean you are tonight's "maybe." Confusing digital attention with real-world value is how women end up overestimating themselves and underestimating men.

App Brain has made you shallow, inflated, impulsive, and unrealistic. Then you complain that men do not commit. Why would they? Swipes are not proposals. Likes are not loyalty. A DM is not devotion. Dating apps are not built to get you married. They are built to keep you addicted, scrolling, swiping, and searching for validation that never lasts. You get matches and situationships, while the app gets your time, energy, hope; and your money.

Dating apps were never designed for men. They were designed to create the illusion that women have endless options. They were built to flatter you, not guide you. And that illusion keeps you coming back for more... 'like a heroin addict. The apps thrive on your dissatisfaction because you swipe more when you are unhappy. They survive by convincing you that your perfect man is just one swipe away.

After watching this chaos, men start asking themselves what marriage even offers anymore. The answer is not complicated. They want calm in a world that already throws enough battles at them. If a woman cannot bring peace, she brings no reason to marry.

App brain has convinced women they have options everywhere. In truth, your terminal case of App Brain has taken away the one thing that should have mattered most to you: reality.

Truth #21 – Men Marry for Peace

Men marry for peace. That is the whole secret. Men are not searching for drama, chaos, or a woman who treats arguments like cardio. They want loyalty, respect, stability, and a quiet place to lay their heads without being interrogated over the tone of a text or why they did not "heart" your last post. When a man says, "I do," he is hoping for a lifelong teammate, not a lifelong headache with eyelashes.

Women, on the other hand, often marry for status. For the wedding photos, the ring they can flash in the group chat, and the social validation that comes from getting a man to commit. They chase aesthetics, money, and appearances so they can say they "made it". Love is optional. Stability is negotiable. The ring must sparkle, the venue must impress, and the wedding hashtag must be flawless.

While men look for peace, many women measure success by the size of their honeymoon and the number of likes on their photos. And when the performance fades, the next chapter is divorce, neatly wrapped in designer victim language about how he was "misogynistic" or "narcissistic."

If you take anything from this book, it is this.

Men marry for peace. Women marry for performance.

And that difference is why men are no longer lining up to walk down that aisle.

Men want an orderly and peaceful home. A peaceful family. A peaceful spouse. Women claim they want those things too, but they do not like the responsibilities that create peace. They choose homes that require constant cleaning and maintenance, then get overwhelmed. They want peaceful children but refuse to discipline them when it interferes with their hobbies or their screen time. They say they want a peaceful man,  then call him boring. Stability is unattractive to them unless it comes with drama on the side.

Women love the bad boys because chaos feels exciting. Peace feels dull. But peace is the foundation of everything men value. And this is where it all connects. Men want partnership.

Women shout for independence. Men offer peace. Women offer chaos.

Men attempt to build, while women demand things from them. Men show up, while women keep performing for everyone around them, except for the man who may actually be interested in them and could be a suitable, reliable husband.

But of course, this has been a problem throughout time. A man likes a woman, but that woman thinks she could do better. In past cultures or cultures like India today, marriage would be arranged by families and last forever. Marriages were not based on "love" or "happiness". But in modernity, the illusion of happiness and choice diminishes the actual purpose of marriage: survival.

Women pushed aside survival, and choose to believe "love" is the purpose of marriage. That illusion is fading and is no longer working for them. What changed is simple. Modern men realized they cannot love you the way you want, and they cannot make you "happy". And then they realized, that they don't "need" you. They "want" partnership, not performance. And once men understood they could live without the stress modern women often bring, the entire balance shifted.

Here is the irony to many western women. If men choose to, they can travel anywhere around the world and marry women who are dirt poor, attractive and physically fit. Those women will be more traditional and conservative. Modern men have options. Western women cannot travel the world to find the men they desire because they will not find the men they want... And still, those men want what Western men want. Peaceful, feminine women!

Truth #22 – You've Forgotten You Need Men

You have been shouting, "I don't need a man," for so long that you eventually believed it. But the reality is that women need men, and deep down, you know it. Men build the world you live in. Men construct the roads, raise the buildings, wire the power, pave the streets, and protect the society that keeps you safe. Every structure you step into, every system you rely on, every piece of modern life you enjoy exists because men created, maintained, and defended it.

Men want women for companionship and family, but they do not need women to survive. We all know a man who lives alone with his dogs; he works alone and builds alone. He eats simple meals, lives in silence, and finds contentment without performing for anyone. We all wonder how he does it, but he seems peaceful.

Women, on the other hand, crave connection and attention like oxygen. That is why you are glued to social media, posting thirst traps for validation from strangers you will never meet. You treat loneliness like a crisis and broadcast it to the masses. When was the last time you saw a man record himself crying on the internet because he is lonely? Exactly. Men deal with isolation. Women advertise it.

Women have forgotten they need men. Not as accessories. Not as backup plans. But as the very foundation of the lives they enjoy. The homes, the protection, the stability, the comfort, the infrastructure, the order, the safety. All of the houses women live in. All of the streets. All of the plumbing. All of the electrical power grid. All of the cars. All of the gas stations. All of the countries on the planet were built by men!

If you doubt this assertion; just **<u>Test yourself and think of 3 things women invented and implemented without men...</u>**

It was a tough question. I get it; 'but understand the question from your future husband's (or your ex-husband's) perspective: If a wife were to treat a husband the way women (in general) treat "men" (in general) within modern western cultures, it would become obvious that their marriage was on the predictable road to divorce.

If you can understand that concept, you should be able to understand that men can understand that concept as well. And they are not going to get married because no one wants to be disrespected, defrauded, or treated unfairly.

    The truth is not complex. Women need Men, and you always have. You rely on the innovations they've created. You need the power they generate that you are using right now, the house that you are living in right now, the roads that you drove on today. and the dangers they confront. With men, the world will keep functioning. You depend on the systems men design and the stability men provide. That is not misogyny. That is the reality of the world!

• • •

That is the end of the 22 Truths.

Each truth stands like a brick in a wall, built from frustration, disappointment, and lessons men learned the hard way. These are explanations, not complaints. This is math, not bitterness. It is an observation, not conspiracy.

Men did not gather together and write these truths as a movement or a manifesto. They lived them. They earned them through silence, through losses, through years of being told they were the problem while quietly keeping score of what went wrong. The 22 Truths are not theories. They are the realities that men stopped arguing about and finally started taking action on.

And here is what many women will find unsettling...

The 22 Truths are not up for debate. They are not meant to be "corrected" by hashtags or a thousand "not all women" disclaimers. These truths are how men see the world. They are the reality he experiences. You can disagree with them. You can dislike them, but you cannot dismiss them without proving the men right!

For years, men listened to every version of what women want: taller, richer, more emotional, better at communicating, more expressive, more stable—more of everything. This is the first time men answered the question in reverse.

Ask yourself: What do men see when they look back? What did they learn from the wreckage of their past relationships?

If these truths feel harsh, it is because they were not filtered to be polite. The point here is not to shame women. The point is to make them aware. You cannot fix what you refuse to admit is broken, and you cannot reach a man you no longer understand. And if a man perceives that you do not understand him, why would he try to build a relationship with you?

Many women have forgotten what men bring to the table and they have lost sight of why the table exists in the first place. Marriage was never about comfort or convenience. It was about purpose. Marriage meant two people working, sacrificing, and building something stronger than their moods. Today, that purpose is blurred, and men have adjusted accordingly. They are not refusing love; they are protecting themselves from loss. They are not afraid of marriage; they are afraid of signing up for a catastrophic failure they can see coming.

So here we are. The wall is built. The distance is real. But the silence between the two sides has never been louder.

Before you defend, deny, deflect, **<u>or start typing a negative book review about toxic masculinity</u>**,

Let's Take a Little Quiz.

The purpose is to see how aware and honest you are with yourself. Nothing serious, but just a few questions. No filters. No captions. No excuses. Just your truth. The quiz has been calibrated to punish answers that are likely untruths. So take the quiz and see what happens.

The Mirror Test

Check off what applies to you. (Be honest with yourself. No one is watching.)

	Do you confuse attention with affection?
	When a relationship ends, do you always blame the man and never admit your own faults?
	Do you crave social media "likes" from strangers?
	Do you expect a man to fix what your attitude keeps breaking? (You never apologize to him.)
	Did you call yourself "independent" but still expect a man to pay for nearly everything you desire (e.g., dates)?
	Do you think sacrifice means skipping brunch, nail, or hair appointments?
	You believe you're "the table" while he's just a resource for you?
	In the past, have you declared that a six-foot, six-figure man with a six-pack is your minimum requirement?
	Do you demand respect from men while mocking them online (i.e., calling them "broke" or "too short")?
	Do you believe happiness means always getting your way?
	Do you expect loyalty from a man while you keep a roster of men in your phone?
	Do you want unconditional love while making your love transactional (e.g., dinner, trips)?
	Do you say you don't need a man, but cry when one won't commit to you?

	Would you expect a man to raise children that are not his?
	Do you chase validation from strangers more than you appreciate the man who shows up?
	Do you think masculinity oppresses women??
	Do you call yourself a queen while treating men like peasants?
	Do you want a man to lead, but only if he follows your rules?
	Do you lie about your past while demanding honesty from men?

Most women will not answer these honestly. It requires self-awareness and accountability, two traits modern culture discourages. But the more questions you check, the more you must accept that men are not your actual problem; it is the woman you see in the mirror.

Count up the questions that may apply to you.

What Is Your Score? _____

If you checked:

0 to 5
*You might be **the Exception**.*

You bring peace, loyalty, and value. Men see wife material in you. You likely grew up around a healthy family or strong role models. You have a balanced sense of self. Men notice it immediately. You are a "wife".

6 to 11
*You are **the Maybe Baby**.*

You could get married, but only if you drop the entitlement, stop fighting peace, and let go of bad advice. You may have rebelled against your upbringing, or you absorbed feminist ideology that turned you hostile toward traditional partnership. You can succeed, but only if you embrace the role of a teammate instead of a competitor to a man.

12 or more
*You are **the Walking Red Flag**.*

You are not wife material. Men will date you. Men will sleep with you. But they will marry someone else. You gravitate toward dysfunctional men because healthy men are boring to you. You are combative, chaotic, and allergic to accountability. Even if someone married you, the marriage would collapse. You cannot be honest with yourself, and therefore, you cannot be honest with a man. No relationship can survive that. ***I am so sorry!***

• • •

If these questions stung, that is a good sign. Growth hurts. Truth cuts. Just about every woman says she wants honesty until she hears it. When she hears something she doesn't like, it is fight or flight. This quiz is not here to shame you but to guide you. Somewhere beneath the noise and the slogans, women still want love, and men still want to give it, but peace must return before connection can.

What you see in the mirror is not judgment. It is the truth. The mirror is always honest. And with that honesty, the future becomes clearer.

Now that you have taken the mirror test, more questions become unavoidable. You should have a better sense of who you are. You can realistically imagine what men see in you. So, the real question for you is not whether you want marriage. The real question is whether marriage is still a realistic outcome for you.

But before anyone starts pointing fingers, the question this book is premised upon is:

"Why won't men marry you?"

A companion question for you **Should Be**...

What Does This All Mean for You?

• • •

The world has never been harsher for men. Every day, a man is competing—at work, in status, in income, in physical expectations, and in social value. Meanwhile, women are handed advantages men will never experience: feminine beauty, social sympathy, and a culture designed to cushion their mistakes while punishing his. Modern society opens doors for women and slams them on men. That imbalance shapes everything, especially marriage.

When a man says, "I do," here is what he is really risking:

- **His money**
- **His future earnings**
- **Child support**
- **Alimony**
- **Attorney fees**
- **His home and assets**
- **His freedom**

Women get social praise for effort. Men get punished for failure. A man can be too masculine or too emotional, too ambitious, or too lazy. No matter what role he plays, society finds a way to blame him. That is the battlefield he walks into. And marriage does not soften that pressure—it **magnifies** it.

Why would any man willingly step into the risk of marriage? He becomes **legally responsible** for his wife's debt, even after a divorce. If he earns more, he pays more in taxes, in court, and in life.

If things fall apart, he watches his ex, post pictures from Cabo and Miami with the "friend" she told him not to worry about. Marriage becomes a constant audit. Every purchase must be justified. Every decision must be approved. Every moment of peace becomes conditional.

His reward?

An adult roommate who withholds intimacy when angry and who guards the thermostat like a medieval gatekeeper.

People say marriage creates stability. Maybe it does, but mostly for **her**.

- If she leaves, she gets the house and the kids.
- If *he* leaves, he gets shamed.
- If she cheats, she blames "emotional needs."
- If he cheats, he is a villain.

Marriage does not give men stability. It puts them under surveillance—and with terrible consequences. Imagine if marriage were pitched as a business deal, and the deal went like this:

> *"You, the man, will provide everything. I, the woman, will provide nothing. If I, the woman, choose to leave because I get bored with the marriage, I will be entitled to take half, keep custody of the kids, and get to stay in the marital home. You, the man, will keep the bills and be required to pay my debt. I may stop contributing halfway through, but you're not allowed to complain. I will keep taking you to court to fight for more money, and spousal support that will last, until I get remarried AND the children turn 18 years of age."*

Would any rational man sign up for that contract? Yet men sign up for it every day. Buying her a $17,000 ring and paying off a $45,000 wedding. Smart men, however, started looking at the data:

- Divorce sits near **50%**.
- Sex declines after marriage.
- Emotional labor increases.
- Courts overwhelmingly side with women.

The financial damage is often catastrophic. You would not drive a car with a 50% chance of exploding. So why sign a contract with the same odds?

That is why men are hesitating. That is why they are walking away. They are done believing the Pinterest fantasy, the staged photoshoots, and the "dream wedding" delusion.

Men are not scared of commitment. They fear **ruin**. Because the woman who shouts, "I don't need a man!" on Instagram is usually the first to treat him like property once the ring slides on.

The Decline Was Predictable

In the 1980s and 1990s, women still believed in partnership. The roles were clearer. There was respect, loyalty, and value on both sides.

By the 2000s and 2010s, everything flipped. "Strong and independent" stopped meaning self-sufficient. It began to mean ego, entitlement, weaponized emotions, and anti-male rhetoric. As that message grew louder, the marriage rate fell off a cliff.

By **2023**, marriage in America hit a historic low: **Only 6.1 marriages per 1,000 people**, according to the Centers for Disease Control (CDC). That is not a dip.

That is a collapse.

At the same time, divorce stayed strong:

- Nearly **50%** of marriages end.
- **70–80%** of divorces are filed by women.

This translates to:

Men are marrying women who are statistically likely to leave them and take half of everything on the way out.

Men are not bitter or angry.

Men are simply **finished**!

They watched their fathers get drained, uncles get destroyed, their brothers get humiliated, and friends get gutted by the system. They saw what the courts do to men. They saw how marriage is used as leverage against them, and they decided:

"No more."

Marriage is optional for women but dangerous for men.

But You Still Want Marriage?

If you still want marriage, you cannot ignore these realities. You cannot dismiss the numbers. You cannot pretend the system is fair when every man can see that it isn't.

You have work to do!
You must unlearn the slogans. You must reject the entitlement script. You must understand what men face and why

they hesitate. Stop shouting that you "don't need a man." Start showing that you *value* one. Start showing you understand what men risk and why that matters.

Men do not hate women. Men dislike nonsense. And they are done signing up for it because the truth is mathematical, not emotional. Between **1999 and 2000**, marriage rates began to fall, and divorce rates fell with them. Not because things improved, but because fewer people married at all.

For every number of marriages formed in a year, roughly half that number will end in divorce.

Men are quietly opting out. They are no longer willing to gamble everything for nothing. And that is the world women now walk in... 'whether they accept it or not.

The number of never-married men in America has more than doubled in the past 40 years. In 1980, 22% of men ages 25–54 had never been married. Today, that number is over 44%.

Source: U.S. Census Bureau, 2022.

After everything you have just read—the 22 Truths, the cultural shifts, the legal risks, the math, the patterns, the realities no one wants to admit—one question floats to the surface.

Not; *"Why won't men marry women?"*
Not; *"Why are men walking away?"*
Not even; *"Why is marriage collapsing?"*

The real question: the only one that matters now is this:

Are *you* ever going to get married?

Not "women" in general.
Not "society."
Not "someone someday."
You! Are **YOU** ever going to get married?

Marriage is no longer presumed "The Norm." It is no longer likely. It is no longer the default path of adulthood. It is a choice, and men have become far more selective about making it. The days of "any woman can get a husband if she wants one" are gone. Men are not lining up. They are not chasing you or proposing just because you turned twenty-eight and your friends told you it was time.

If you want marriage, *you have to qualify for it.* And that means looking inward, not outward.

This next chapter is not about blaming men, blaming culture, or blaming your ex. It is about facing the hardest question a modern woman can ask herself:

Given everything men now know, everything they've seen, everything they risk, and everything they observe women do… why would a man choose *you*?

Why Would a Man Choose You?

• • •

You have two choices. You can close this book and convince yourself that none of this applies to you, or you can stand in front of the mirror and tell the truth. Every woman believes she is the exception. Every woman thinks she is different. But behavior, patterns, and their outcomes do not lie. If men keep saying the same things about you, and if your results keep repeating, maybe it is not a vast conspiracy. Maybe the mirror is finally talking.

It should be obvious, but men are not going to marry a woman just because she wants it. The ring is not a participation trophy. Being a husband or a wife is not just for your social media relationship updates. It is a role. And like any role, it comes with responsibility, consistency, and sacrifice.

This is where countless modern women fail. They want the title of "wife", without the labor. They want the perks of being a wife. The ring, the wedding, the status, and the pictures. But they do not want the discipline or duty that makes marriage work.

Men have noticed. No man wants to marry someone who refuses to do the job. No company hires an employee who will not work. Marriage is no different. If you cannot deliver on the role, you should not expect the title.

If you are still reading, congratulations. It means you want the thing most men are actively avoiding: marriage. After reviewing the 22 Truths, one fact is undeniable. If you want to be chosen, you must be the exception, not the rule.

What does that mean in real life? It means that if you want to be a wife, you must do two things:

1. "Understand" the 22 Truths, and
2. Date at your actual level.

Your Level

There are levels to the dating game, and who marries whom follows a pattern as predictable as gravity. The men with the most resources usually pair with the women who are the most attractive. That is why a short, older, or balding man can walk into a restaurant with a woman who looks like she belongs on a magazine cover. The first thing people say when they see it is "He must have money."

Otherwise, what biologists call **ASSORTATIVE MATING** is the rule. Translation: people tend to partner with their equals. Fat men end up with fat women. Fit men end up with fit women. Tall people find tall people. Poor finds poor. The same happens with age, education, and status. Everyone wants to date up, but most pair across.

But women try to avoid and ignore assortative mating. They do not want their assortative match. Instead, they chase men with money, who are better looking than they are. They expect him to be fit, successful, and have a high social status. They will talk about "chemistry" all day, but when a wealthy man arrives, the chemistry magically shows up too.

Rating Yourself (on a 1–10 scale)

With levels comes the rating system. Picture the classic Bell Curve. A 1 and 10 are rare. Most people sit in the middle. But women do not grade themselves by the curve. They grade themselves by feelings.

A woman who is a 6 will insist she is a nine because 10 thirsty men said "hey beautiful" on Instagram. A woman who is a 5 will claim she is a ten because her friends scream "yasss queen" after she posts a filtered selfie. Women grade emotionally. Men grade realistically.

Men understand the curve. They know a 6 is solid. They know a 7 is attractive. They know a 10 is rare and a 5 is normal. Most men and women fall between 4 and 7. That is the reality of it. The ends of the curve are unicorn territory. If you are calling yourself a 9 or 10 without the evidence, you are grading yourself on delusion.

A fair way to begin is to assume you are a 5. From there, your habits, discipline, choices, and personality raise or lower your rating **<u>TO A MAN</u>**.

Here is the truth:

When it comes to men's resources or women's looks, most people land around the average. Which means if you are holding out for a 10 while you rate at a 5, you are not waiting for Prince Charming. You are waiting for disappointment. Look at the Bell Curve below. See that middle hump? That is where most people stand in the Bell Curve. Not in the fantasy land of 10s or the tragic basement of 1s, but in the wide, ordinary middle of 4 to 7. That is reality.

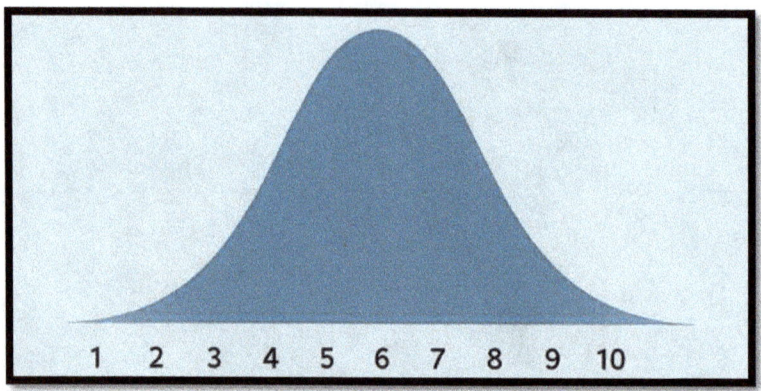

The Bell Curve does not lie. In any population, both 1s and 2s, as well as 9s and 10s, are exceedingly rare... Just like rich men are rare. Women with top-tier beauty are not on every city corner. The majority of people are average. Average does not mean worthless; it means normal. Most men and women fall in the realistic middle, and it is not a bad thing!

The 10s stand out in a way that everyone who sees them do double takes. They are amazing-looking, but that doesn't stop average (mid) women from declaring themselves 9s or 10s, while ignoring the scale entirely. Truth be told, you are likely NOT above average. You are just grading yourself on delusion. **I'm sorry, but you are NOT a 9 or 10.**

The only assumption that can be made is that women overrate themselves and their friends.

Men use the Bell Curve, while women use a magic mirror. When men rate women, it is simple. Looks, youth, femininity, peace. If you are a 6, you are a 6. If you are an 8, you are an 8. Men are not afraid of numbers, and they know a 7 is great. That is why men will happily date a 4 or 5 or lower if that man rates himself around that same range. And if a woman brings loyalty and peace? Men will rate her higher.

Women? Not so much. Women do not see the Bell Curve. They see feelings. She thinks she is an 8 because one guy in her inbox told her she was a queen. She thinks she is a 9 because her friends tell her she is a "Boss Babe" every time she posts a filtered selfie. She thinks she is a 10 because her best friends tell her she is even though the dating market and reality says otherwise. Women rate themselves based on attention, not outcomes. They confuse likes for value and validation for reality.

If men judged themselves the way women do, every guy at the bar would swear he is Brad Pitt. But men cannot fake it. Their bank accounts, height, and status expose them instantly. Women, on the other hand, can hide behind filters, makeup, and saying dumb statements like, "I am working on myself," while still insisting they are a 10.

The Bell Curve stands as a brutal reminder that women are not what they *feel* they are. Women are what the market decides they are. Men are the market that determines if a woman is a 2, a 4, or a 10.

A general method to determine what you are without a board of men judging you is to start with the presumption that you are a 5; that you are dead center on the Bell Curve. From there, you move up or down based on your qualities, your choices, and your habits.

What Men Notice and Appreciate

- **Fitness and Health:** Staying in shape shows discipline. Would a man say you're fit and in shape?
- **Femininity:** Men do not marry competition. Softness and loyalty raise your value. Are you feminine?
- **Style and Presentation:** You do not need luxury brands. Clean and intentional goes a long way. Is that you?
- **Accountability:** Owning mistakes is rare. Rare is valuable. Are You Rare?
- **Respect and Support:** Men invest in women who invest in them. Are you respectful, and respectable?

It is important for you to note that your rating is subjective. Society may judge you in general as average, mid, or a 5, but that is because you are being judged in general by your looks. But... to an individual man, who knows you and has wanted to learn more about you, you may be a "10" *IN HIS EYES*. One guy may see you and want to spend his life with you.

What Men Notice and <u>DO NOT</u> Appreciate

- **Entitlement and Attitude:** Do you believe you "deserve better" than every man you've been in a relationship with?
- **Chaos and Drama:** Have you ever been told your life is like a soap opera? Men hate soap operas, they like peace!
- **High Body Count:** It matters. Every man knows it, even if he will not say it out loud. No man wants to marry that...
- **Disrespect:** Tear down men, play the victim, or dodge accountability, and you will sink fast.
- **Do you blame men?:** Are all your issues due to men (your father included?
- **Do you have kids?:** and expect a man who's not the father to assume more responsibility than the biological father?

This is not perfect science. **This is highly subjective**, but it is a framework. Women tend to rate themselves through emotion. Reality requires structure. If you doubt this, think of your closest circle of single friends, especially the ones who are hard to deal with and hostile. You may still rate them as 8s, 9s, or 10s because you love them, but men don't seem to agree.

Again, most women are not 9s or 10s. But if you can reach a solid 6 or 7, you are already above the curve. Be proud of it.

Don't Confuse Attention with Desire

Knowing where you land on the curve is only half the battle. The other half is proving that you possess the qualities that make a man choose to marry you. When a man does choose to marry you, he's not thinking it it's temporary. He's thinking it it's for life. He used to understand the risks of divorce, but now, modern men are not willing to take that risk any longer.

Due to the nature of men, they will show attention to just about any woman whether she rates a 4 out of 10, or a 9. Men will look, and if a 3 is all he has access to, he may even give her attention, especially if he's been drinking... BUT!!! He doesn't desire her. And he would never marry her.

Women have a tendency to confuse the fact that a man is giving her attention as a clue that he desires her. No. In fact, men have a saying. It goes like this:

"For every hot girl out there, there's a man who is tired of her bullshit!"

So, to answer the question of, "Are You Gonna Marry?"

The answer is that if you cannot rate yourself effectively and search for men on your level...

No! You're likely NOT going to marry!

Why Men Won't Marry You

20 Tenets to Marriage

• • •

If you are still reading, you want something most women talk about but very few are willing to work for. You want a marriage that lasts. That already puts you ahead of the women who complain about men while never asking what men actually want. By choosing to keep going, you demonstrate that you are serious about becoming the rare woman who stands out.

You have read the <u>22 Truths.</u> They explained why men hesitate to marry. You now know that men do not fear commitment. They fear regret. Men do not fear love, but they do fear being drained by someone who brings stress and chaos. Men are not avoiding marriage because they hate women. They avoid it because they struggle to find women who bring stability, loyalty, and respect. If you want marriage, you must show that you are different from the rest.

That is where the **20 Tenets** come in. These are not tricks, slogans, or dating hacks. They are not shortcuts, and they are not designed to get you quick attention. These tenets are principles that change the way a man experiences you. Each tenet shows a prospective husband that you are safe to trust, safe to build with, and safe to love.

Think of these tenets as your roadmap. They move you from desiring marriage to preparing for it. They help you prove that you are not just another woman shouting that you *deserve* a ring, but that you are a woman who understands partnership. A woman who brings calm instead of chaos. A woman who chooses loyalty over games and respect over attitude.

When you practice these tenets, you separate yourself from the pack. Looks may draw a man in, but character is what keeps him. These tenets build that character. They lift your value in a world where entitlement is common and accountability is rare.

These tenets are not about lowering yourself. It is about raising your standards. It is about proving that you deserve the life you want because you are willing to do the work. Most women want the "wife" title, but very few want the responsibility that comes with it.

Many women have shown that they can get a proposal. Very few can keep a marriage. These 20 Tenets will help you do both. They teach you how to earn a man's respect, protect his trust, and build a bond that lasts. Men are not looking for perfect women. They are looking for peaceful, loyal, and stable women. These tenets help you become exactly that.

Take them seriously. If you apply them with honesty and effort, you will not only increase your chances of marriage but will also create a marriage worth keeping. The goal is not the ring. The goal is the life that comes after it.

Here are the 20 Tenets.

• • •

Tenet 1
Drop the "I Don't Need a Man"

You said it with pride. Men heard it clearly, then took a step back.

For years, women have been taught that declaring independence is a sign of power and that needing a man is weakness. That message created a generation of women who brag about not needing men and a generation of men who realized there was no place for them.

When a woman insists she does not need a man, she should not be shocked when men believe her.

Men do not marry women who act self-sufficient to the point of hostility. Men marry women who make space for them. Men want to feel needed, valued, and respected. They want to know their presence matters. When you tell the world that you need nothing from a man, you remove the very role that makes him feel like a husband.

Independence is healthy until it becomes arrogance. Confidence is attractive. Pride isolates. You can be strong, capable, and successful while still showing that you appreciate a man's effort. Men do not commit to women who make them feel like competition. They commit to women who show partnership.

If you want a man, act like you want one. Appreciation. Cooperation. Respect. Modern men are done fighting for relevance in relationships that feel like contests. You do not prove strength by pretending you can do everything on your own. You prove wisdom by allowing a good man to do what men naturally do. A man leads, protects, and provides. When you reject that role, you are also rejecting him.

Drop the line. It is not a badge of empowerment.

It is a warning label and a red flag that tells men to stay away.

Tenet 2
Control Your Mouth

A woman's mouth can destroy more than any weapon. It can wreck peace, drain a man's spirit, and turn a home into a battlefield. Men do not marry chaos. They avoid it. Constant yelling, nagging, sarcasm, and disrespect do not show strength. They show a lack of discipline. A sharp tongue may win the argument, but it will lose the man. If you are dating him, he will never propose. If you are married to him, the marriage will not last.

Respect is not optional. It is the foundation of every healthy relationship. The way you speak to a man determines whether he feels valued or undermined. A woman who cannot control her tone is not ready for commitment. A man should feel peace in his home, not hostility. He should feel respected, not managed, or scolded.

Men do not see emotional outbursts as passion. They see them as instability. What you call expression, he experiences as exhaustion.

When every disagreement becomes a spectacle, a man stops engaging. He withdraws, he shuts down, and eventually he leaves. Not because he is weak, but because no man wants to live under verbal fire.

Men also remember what you say when you are angry. They may forgive, but they do not forget the disrespect. Every insult chips away at trust. Every harsh word weakens the connection. Over time, the relationship collapses under the weight of unrestrained emotion.

If you want to be a wife, learn to pause. Think before you speak. Ask yourself whether your words bring peace or poison. A wise woman builds her home with her voice. A foolish woman tears it down with her own mouth.

Control your mouth, and you will control the tone of your relationship.

Tenet 3
Get Fit AND Stay Fit

Men are visual. They always have been, and they always will be. You do not need to look like a model, but you cannot look like someone who stopped trying. A woman who respects herself takes care of herself. Fitness is not vanity. It is discipline. It shows effort, self-control, and pride. It signals to a man that you value your health, your appearance, and the relationship you hope to build.

A man notices when a woman is committed to staying attractive. He also notices when she has given up. Men are not inspired by excuses. They are inspired by effort. Women love to say, "He should love me as I am," but they expect him to keep working, earning, building, and providing. If you want him to keep his standards high, yours must be high as well.

The truth is clear. Men are drawn to women who take care of themselves. A fit woman sends a message without ever speaking. She shows she can commit, has structure in her life, and is capable of consistency. Those are qualities that make a strong partner and a strong wife.

Getting fit is not about competing with other women. It is about proving you can maintain what you attract. A man wants to know that the woman he meets today is the same woman he will see ten years from now. He wants to know that you will not abandon yourself the moment you feel comfortable. Effort is not optional, so if you want a man to invest in you for life, show him that you invest in yourself.

Get fit and stay fit. Attraction may begin with looks, but it survives on discipline.

From August 2021 to August 2024, the Centers for Disease Control and Prevention (CDC) within the United States identified:

- **40.3% of Americans above age 20 were classified as obese (a Body Mass Index (BMI) greater than 30)**

Tenet 4
Get Off Social Media

Give it a rest. Men do not want their private lives turned into public entertainment. If you cannot choose between your man and your followers, the truth is that your man will choose neither. No man wants to compete with strangers on a screen for your attention, and no marriage survives when online validation matters more than loyalty at home.

Social media has led women to believe that they have an endless supply of rich men who own yachts and take women they just met on shopping sprees for expensive clothes, luxury shoes, and designer handbags. Women see it on social media and think they can be the next woman it happens to. They begin to think they can go "viral" and then "monetize" their social media accounts. But in reality, they find that nothing is working out for them. Then the disappointment sets in, which turns into jealousy. The jealousy festers over time and they become frustrated with men.

Women are not upset that men are not approaching them. They are upset that the men ***they want*** are not approaching them. Men have learned that women only want attention from the men they desire, not from the men who desire them. The problem is that most of the men they desire are above average, and most women are not. Average women, therefore, naturally end up with average men. It has always worked that way.

But social media has tricked many women into believing they have endless options, but those options exist only in their imaginations. Online attention is not commitment and comments on the internet, do not equate to interest. Messages are not proposals and regardless of what they say; men who comment or send messages to you, would NEVER marry you. The men you want in real life are not impressed by what you post online. They are actually watching and quietly eliminating you from their list of possibilities.

Few men want to see their girlfriends, let alone their wives, posting family business or spicy pictures online for all to see. If you want real attention, stop chasing fake validation. Get off social media. Step into the real world where conversations matter, where presence counts, and where respect still has value. A man cannot build a life with a woman whose identity lives on her phone.

Real life is where real relationships start. You have to turn off the noise. Especially if you want a man to marry you.

Tenet 5
Stop Chasing the Top 20%

If you are average, do not expect elite outcomes. The fantasy "6-6-6 man" six feet tall, six-pack abs, and six-figure income exists, but he is rare. He is also spoiled for choice. Women do not seem to understand this. They assume that because they want him, he would want them back. That is not how reality works.

Almost all women desire the top 20% of men. They are tall, fit, successful, and attractive. What woman would not want a man like that? The problem is simple. Only 20% of men fit that category, which means most women are competing for a small group of men who women constantly approach.

You do not get to "manifest" a man simply because you want him. Attraction is not spiritual. It is competitive.

Ask yourself a real question. Why should an above-average man who is disciplined, financially stable, and in shape, care about the approval of a "below-average" or even "average" woman? Why should he settle for anything less than an above-average partner as he is? He earned his value. He built it through work, sacrifice, risk, and consistency. He has options because he created them.

The higher a man climbs, the larger his dating pool becomes, and the more selective he becomes. That is not arrogance. That is selection. The same way a woman wants the best man, a high-value man wants the best woman he can get. But understand that women, are higher value when they are younger, fitter, and more feminine. If a 24 years old woman is working as a waitress, but is nice, gorgeous and feminine, she can date a millionaire.

You do not see top-tier men settling for women who are unfit, disrespectful, combative, or "average". Men at the top want peace, beauty, femininity, and loyalty. They will not compromise on those qualities because they do not have to. So the question is quite simple:

What makes you part of the top 20% of women that these men might want?

It is not your attitude. Not your excuses. Not your desires. Not your social media followers. And definitely not your self-declared rating. You need to seriously consider that question. Because until you stop chasing men who do not want you, you will overlook the very men who you could build a real life with.

Date in your league. Support and grow with a man who sees your value. The man who builds with you will remember your loyalty long after the fantasy fades.

Tenet 6
Kill the Entitlement

Entitlement destroys attraction. Gratitude keeps it alive. A man can instantly tell the difference between a woman who appreciates effort and a woman who demands it. One inspires him to give more. The other convinces him to give nothing at all.

A man notices when a woman expects everything and offers nothing in return. He also notices when she appreciates what he gives freely. Generosity only feels good when it is voluntary. The moment a woman expects it, the kindness becomes a bill, and no man wants to pay one for the rest of his life.

Do not expect a man to pay for everything, especially when he is only dating you. If he offers, accept it with gratitude. If you demand it, you turn generosity into obligation. And obligation kills romance faster than rejection ever will.

Women often forget that love is supposed to go both ways. Men are not on this planet to serve you, finance you, or constantly entertain you. They have needs, hopes, and limits just like you do. Relationship success requires reciprocity. If you want a man to value you, he must feel valued too.

If a man senses that your affection comes with a price tag, he loses interest in paying it. Why would he want to marry someone who treats his effort like a requirement instead of a gift?

Entitlement today becomes resentment tomorrow. Men know this, which is why they avoid it.

The women who stand out in today's world are the ones who say, "thank you," not "finally." Gratitude is rare now, and that rarity makes it powerful. A woman who appreciates a man will receive more from him than a woman who treats him like a credit card with legs.

Kill the entitlement. Build gratitude. That shift alone makes you unforgettable.

Tenet 7
Respect His Leadership

Most women do not want to hear this, but they need to: a relationship cannot function without a leader, and in a healthy marriage, that leader is the man. This is not oppression. It is not patriarchy. It is nature operating the same way it always has. In nearly every mammal species on Earth, the male leads, protects, and absorbs danger so the family can survive. Humans are not an exception. We are part of that same design.

A man thinks differently than you do. He sees risks you ignore. He considers outcomes you overlook. He protects you in ways you never notice. His leadership is not an attempt to control you. It is the fulfillment of the role nature has given him. When he tells you not to buy an $8,000 purse on credit, that is not domination. It is guidance. When he tells you not to jog alone at night, that is not insecurity. It is protection. Respect that difference.

Modern culture has lied to women, convincing them that leadership is a threat instead of a blessing. Cooperation and submission have been turned into insults, even though every successful relationship is built on them. You cannot build a partnership if you insist on being the captain of a ship that is not designed for two steering wheels. One leads. One supports. That is how marriages survive.

A man leads at his best when he knows his woman trusts him. A woman brings peace when she works with him instead of competing against him. When you respect his leadership, you give him the confidence to take on the hard battles and shoulder the weight that life demands from him. He becomes stronger because you are beside him, not against him.

A wise woman does not challenge her man's authority. She complements it. She brings balance to his strength and calm to his storm. Respecting his leadership is not weakness. It is wisdom. It is the key that unlocks the partnership men are looking for and the stability marriage requires.

Respect his leadership, and he will become the kind of man who leads you, protects you, and builds a life worth sharing.

Tenet 8
Recommend and Sign a Prenup

If you want a man to trust you, protect him with a prenuptial agreement. Bring it up yourself. Draft it. Sign it. Mean it. Nothing tells a man "I love you for you" better than saying, "I am not here for your things." A woman who signs without hesitation proves she values the relationship, not the resources. That kind of loyalty is rare, and rare is priceless.

Men are not avoiding marriage. They are avoiding divorce. They have watched men lose homes, savings, children, and freedom because the legal system is designed to protect women at the expense of men. A smart woman understands this before she ever asks for a ring. She realizes she is not entitled to a man's money or assets if the marriage ends. Yet the system will hand them to her anyway. Men know this, and women should also understand it.

It is unfortunate, but true. Men live under a legal structure where one accusation can ruin their lives. A woman can call the police, make a claim with no evidence, and a man can be arrested on the spot. That is real privilege. And in the face of that reality, women still expect men to trust them blindly. Trust cannot survive when the risk is all on one side.

If you genuinely want marriage, show him that you understand the danger he faces by choosing you. Bring him the prenup before he asks for it. That single act tells him you are different. It tells him you understand the weight he carries and that you are willing to share it. It tells him you want to be his wife, not his liability.

A woman who offers protection earns commitment. A woman who signs a prenup without argument earns trust. And a woman who understands the risk earns the ring.

According to a September 2023 Axios-Harris Poll:

- 50% of US Adults said they were "Somewhat Supportive" of signing prenuptial agreements prior to marriage.

The same poll notes that an ever-increasing 20% of those polled had a prenuptial agreement in place within their own marriages.

Tenet 9
Bring Peace, Not Pressure

Men do not need perfection. They need peace.

A man's home should be his refuge, not another battlefield. When he walks through the door, he is looking for calm, not conflict. He wants to feel safe with the woman he chose, not stressed by her emotions, demands, or attitude. A peaceful woman resets his spirit. A confrontational woman drains it.

Pressure kills love faster than time. Constant arguing, criticism, and unrealistic expectations turn a relationship into labor. Men already fight the world every day. They refuse to come home and fight their wives too.

Stop searching for "your person." Men are not your person. Men are their own person, and you are your own person. A marriage is not two people becoming one. It is two individuals learning how to cooperate, communicate, and compromise without trying to complete each other. Completion is fantasy. Cooperation is reality.

Peace is what separates wives from girlfriends. A wife understands that peace is her power. She knows when to speak and when to listen. She brings balance instead of tension. She does not try to win every argument because she knows that winning the moment can mean losing the man.

Men run and hide from women who bring tension instead of tranquility. If you can bring a man peace, he will protect you, provide for you, and stay loyal without ever being asked.

A peaceful woman is unforgettable. Every man who has known one remembers her his entire life. Every man who has not known one, is searching for her.

If you bring peace, and not pressure, it is the difference between being tolerated and being treasured.

Tenet 10
Take Accountability

Stop blaming men for everything that goes wrong in your life.

Accountability is not punishment. It is actual empowerment. It is the strength to look in the mirror and say, "I'm responsible for this part." That level of honesty separates a grown woman from a perpetual victim.

Men marry women who can own their mistakes. They run from women who turn every conflict into someone else's fault. When a man sees that you can admit when you are wrong, he sees a woman he can trust. When he sees that you always play the victim, he knows he will spend his life defending himself against you.

Excuses are easy. Growth is hard. Every time you say, "Men are trash," you broadcast that you have learned nothing from your choices. Accountability means asking yourself why you chose the men you chose, why you stayed as long as you did, and what red flags you ignored because they suited your feelings at the time.

Obviously, it goes without saying that men are in no way perfect, but they respect women who take responsibility. A woman who says, "I made a mistake," commands more respect than one who rewrites every story to make herself the hero and every man the villain.

Stop editing your past to protect your ego. Use it to elevate your future.

Whether it is fair or not, men believe that accountability is rare for women. You may have heard the jokes and comments about women and accountability. Just understand that anything rare is valuable, so be the woman who admits her mistakes, makes adjustments, and improves by accepting accountability for her words, behaviors, and actions. That is the kind of woman who men want to build a future with.

Tenet 11
Understand His Nature

Men are wired to pursue, build, and conquer. That instinct is not toxic. It is the same force that built every bridge, city, invention, and civilization. The energy that drives a man to chase goals is the same energy that makes him chase you. It is his nature. Respect it.

Commitment is not automatic for men. It is chosen. When a man commits to one woman, he is choosing loyalty over instinct, discipline over impulse, and responsibility over freedom. That decision deserves respect, not interrogation. Now that does not guarantee that he will never fail to meet the highest standards you may expect, but he will be loyal to his wife and family. Especially when he is respected and supported. He will not be perfect, but he will be committed to you.

If you think you will find a perfect man, you are searching for a myth. The man who appears perfect is either lying or hiding. Real men are not flawless. They are consistent, honest, and loyal (to their relationships) despite their imperfections. Expecting perfection is the fastest way to sabotage a relationship with a man who would have given you the world.

Now. This is going to be tough to hear. But many women will read the word "loyal" and laugh because of the repeated experiences they may have had with a man who had a "wondering eye". It is an unfortunate part of nature that men are wired this way! But consider this truth. Even when married men stray from a "good wife", it was not to wreck their marriages. It was a physical act and if the wife never found out, the marriage would survive until one of them dies. Men may look for sex, but women look for a possible replacement to fall in love with.

Men are not machines. They are visual, driven, and competitive by design. Shame those traits and you weaken the very qualities that make men capable of protecting, providing, and loving. Respect those traits and you unlock the best version of the man beside you.

Women often mistake a man's discipline for weakness. They think a man who stays faithful is simply doing the bare minimum, when in reality, he is doing what is hardest for him. A man resists temptation out of respect for the woman he loves. When that sacrifice is ignored or dismissed, he begins to wonder why he even bothers trying.

Understand what a man is, before demanding what he should be. When you stop treating masculinity as a threat, you begin to see it as the protection and strength it truly is for you and a possible future family.

Tenet 12
Keep Your Body Count Low

It matters. It always has.

You can deny it, argue it, or shame men for caring, but none of that changes male nature. Men care about a woman's past because a woman's past reveals her patterns. Patterns show whether she values loyalty, self-control, and commitment. A high body count is not a badge of empowerment. It signals impulsiveness, instability, and emotional damage that accumulates over time.

A high body count does not make you experienced. It makes you common. Exclusivity is valuable. What is rare is respected, while sharing too freely loses its worth. Men know this instinctively because they value women who reserve intimacy for the man they choose to build a future with.

Modern culture encourages women to "explore," "experiment," and "live their truth," but it conveniently avoids mentioning the cost. Every man is aware of the truth that biology refuses to hide. Women form bonds through intimacy because of the hormones, dopamine, and oxytocin. The hormones are released as women, and men, bond with other humans. Every time that bond forms and then breaks, the next bond becomes weaker. Too many partners make long-term attachment harder, which is why women with higher body counts struggle with loyalty, stability, and long-term pair bonding.

Men do not want to compete with a woman's past. They want to feel chosen. They do not want ghosts in the room or memories they can never erase. When a man is thinking about marriage, he wants a woman whose intimacy still means something, not someone who treats it like a hobby.

You cannot change how men are wired. You can only choose how you live. Protect your value, protect your future, and protect your ability to bond with a man you may want to marry. A low body count is not about shame. It is about respect for yourself and the relationship you hope to build.

Tenet 13
Know the Role of a Wife

Marriage is not a free-for-all. It has structure, purpose, and roles. There is a husband, and there is a wife. When those roles are ignored or blended into one, the relationship loses its direction, and the bond begins to fracture.

Men do not want or need a "partner." They want a wife. A partner competes. A wife cooperates. A partner fights for power. A wife works for peace. When a wife tries to play both the masculine and feminine roles, it creates confusion, tension, and eventually distance. Men do not respond well to rivalry inside their own homes.

You are allowed to be a modern woman. You can chase independence, status, and the illusion that equality means sameness. But understand this: the type of man a woman wants most; does not want a modern woman. High-value men choose women who understand balance. They choose women who embrace femininity, bring calm, respect leadership, and create a traditional home worth protecting.

A wife adds value when she supports, nurtures, builds, and brings stability. She multiplies what a man provides, not drains it away with entitlement, disrespect, or emotional chaos. If your idea of being a wife is enjoying the benefits without carrying the responsibilities, you are not prepared for marriage.

Marriage is not oppression. It is structure. It only works when both people respect their roles and fulfill them. When either person abandons their role, the relationship becomes conflict instead of cooperation. If you want to be a wife, learn the role. Honor it. Live it. That is what makes a man commit for life.

"Husband" is a role!

"Wife" is a role!

You can deny those roles if you want, but understand that if you do, that marriage probably will not work, because the roles need to be filled in a successful marriage.

Tenet 14
Stay Feminine

Masculine men are drawn to feminine women. That truth has never changed and never will.

Femininity is not weakness. It is strength in a form men respond to instinctively. It softens his edges, inspires his effort, and makes him want to protect, provide, and commit. When a woman trades her softness for hardness, she does not gain power. She loses the attention of the very men she desires.

Modern culture tells women to act like men in order to prove equality. Compete. Dominate. Assert. Demand. But the men you want already have those traits. He does not need a challenge or a rival at home. He needs a balance.

Femininity is not submission. It is influence. A feminine woman can calm a man with her presence. Her tone, her patience, and her warmth. She can create an environment that makes him want to stay, give, and invest. A man may build the structure, but it is her femininity that turns it into a home.

If you act like a competitor, do not be surprised if he treats you like one. Men are not intimidated by masculine women. They are uninterested in them. They do not want to fight the world only to come home and fight their wife too.

Femininity is not just how you look. It is your energy, your attitude, your peace. A feminine woman stands out instantly because she brings what the modern world is starving for: softness, grace, and calm.

Stay feminine. It is not a performance. It is the quiet strength that turns a man's effort into devotion.

"She had become a woman: not in shape alone, but in spirit, subtle, elusive. Men noticed it when she passed by."

D.H. Lawrence

Tenet 15
Keep Him Satisfied in the Boudoir

Sex is not a reward. It is a requirement.

For men, intimacy is how they feel loved, valued, and grounded in the relationship. It is far more than a physical act. It is affirmation. It tells him he is wanted, respected, and appreciated. When a man feels desired by his woman, he feels connected. When he feels rejected, he feels alone, even while lying next to her.

A woman who withholds sex to punish or control is not building a marriage. She is destroying one. Turning intimacy into a bargaining chip teaches a man that her affection has conditions. Once that idea settles in, trust begins to break. Desire turns into resentment. A man who spends his nights being avoided will eventually stop reaching out altogether.

Men do not want perfection. They want willingness. They want a woman who still touches them, still initiates, and still sees them as her man. A wife who understands this keeps the bond alive long after the early excitement fades.

Men have simple needs, but they notice everything. They remember how you made them feel when you wanted them. They also remember when you stopped trying.

Sex is not just another part of marriage. It is the pulse of it. Neglect it, and you will watch your connection collapse. Nurture it, and you will watch your man become more loyal, more giving, and more devoted than you ever imagined.

Keep him satisfied, and you will keep him committed.

Tenet 16
Respect His Time and Space

Have you ever wondered why men sit in their cars for a couple of minutes before they come inside when they get home from work? Have you been curious why men don't call or text you immediately after you text him? Have you ever wondered why all your married friends tell you that when a man walks into the house, you should just say hello and wait a while before you start talking about your day or asking questions about his day?

Well, that is because men need space and time to recover, and refocus. That is not a flaw. It is how they stay grounded and strong enough to keep showing up for you. A man's quiet is not a sign that he has lost interest. It is usually a sign that he is recharging. Men process their stress internally. They solve problems by stepping back, not by talking them to death. Silence, solitude, and purpose are how men reset.

Men deal with issues throughout the day without speaking to anyone about those problems. When you interrupt that process, you disrupt the peace he needs to protect and provide. Constant questioning, checking in, or demanding emotional updates do not bring him closer. It pushes him into retreat.

Clinging does not create connection. It creates suffocation. A wise woman knows when to speak and when to step back. Giving him space does not mean losing him. It means trusting him.

It shows maturity, security, and confidence in his loyalty.

Men are drawn to women who understand balance. When you give him time to breathe, you give him room to miss you. When you respect his space, you remind him that peace lives with you, not away from you.

If you treat his alone time like betrayal, he will eventually hide from you. If you treat it like rest, he will always return to you.

Respect his time and space. A man who finds peace in your presence will never want to be anywhere else.

Tenet 17
Cut the Sisterhood Nonsense

Your friends do not get a vote in your relationship.

If you let the opinions of single, bitter, or jealous women guide you, do not be surprised when you end up just like them. The same women who hype your independence will be nowhere to be found when you are alone. The same ones who push you to "leave him" will not help you pay your bills, protect your home, or raise your children. Their advice costs them nothing, but it could cost you everything.

Men do not marry women who live for female approval. They marry women who protect the relationship from outside noise. Every time you drag the group chat into your private life, you weaken his trust. No man wants to compete with your friends for authority in his own home.

Sisterhood loyalty should never outrank loyalty to the man you claim to love. Your marriage is not a committee. It is a team of two. Every secret you share, argument you broadcast, and private detail you leak becomes a weapon that can be used against your future peace.

If your friends always have negative things to say about men, it is because no good men want them. Stop taking guidance from people who cannot keep what you are trying to build.

A wise woman protects her relationship. A foolish woman performs for an audience. Choose peace over peer pressure, and you will keep both your man and your dignity.

Tenet 18
Heal Before You Deal

He is not your therapist or your father. He is not responsible for the damage other men left behind.

If you enter a relationship without healing, you will make a good man pay for pain he did not cause. That is not love. It is emotional debt. No man can build a future with a woman still living in the ruins of her past.

Healing is not optional. It is preparation. You cannot attract stability while carrying chaos. You cannot be trusted when you are fighting invisible battles that spill into every argument, every suspicion, and every moment of closeness you desire with a man.

Take time to fix yourself before you offer yourself. Go to therapy. Forgive your past. Release your bitterness. The man who chooses you deserves a clean slate, not a constant reminder of someone else's mistakes.

Men are not afraid of love. They are afraid of women who weaponize pain. A woman who has not healed will mistake kindness for weakness and leadership for control. She will sabotage peace because dysfunction feels normal and stability feels strange.

Do the work before you seek the reward. A healed woman loves better, listens better, and receives love without fear.

Heal before you deal. The man you want deserves the version of you that is ready, not the version that is recovering.

Tenet 19
Stop Chasing Happiness

Modern women chase happiness like it is oxygen. The problem is that happiness is temporary. It rises and falls with emotions, circumstances, and convenience. You cannot build a marriage on something that changes every week.

Men do not chase happiness in marriage. They chase peace. A man does not need constant excitement. He needs stability, respect, and quiet. He wants a partner who brings calm, not chaos, and only when he has those things, that is when he'll begin to feel alive and valued. But when a woman makes peace impossible, he begins to withdraw from her.

Happiness is about what you feel. Peace is about what you create. A peaceful home can survive bad days, boredom, and the natural routines of life. A home built only on "feeling happy" will collapse the moment the excitement fades.

Women today will destroy a marriage over the smallest things. Many walk away because they are bored. Bored in bed. Bored with routine. Bored because the spark dimmed, and they mistake comfort for emptiness. They decide something is wrong simply because it no longer feels exciting.

Past generations of women were stronger. They understood that love was not a constant feeling of stomach "butterflies". It was commitment through boredom, fatigue, and repetition. They stayed when it stopped feeling new because they valued stability over thrill.

Men have been bored in marriage since the beginning of time, yet most do not leave. Husbands get tired, frustrated, and restless, but they stay and continue building. They honor the promise. That is the difference between emotional impulse and steady devotion.

If you want a lasting marriage, stop chasing a feeling and start protecting the peace. Happiness will come and go. Peace is what keeps the marriage standing when happiness runs out.

Tenet 20
Be Exceptional

Do not aim to be average. The average woman complains, competes, and blames. The exceptional woman builds, supports, and improves. Aim to be Exceptional!

A man does not commit to potential. He commits to proof. Show wife qualities before you ever expect a ring. No one gets hired without a résumé, and no man marries without evidence of value. If you bring nothing before the ring, do not be surprised when the ring never comes.

Exceptional women are not born. They are built through consistency, humility, and discipline. They take responsibility for their attitude, energy, and growth. They are not swayed by trends or groupthink. They understand that peace, femininity, and respect never go out of style.

Men remember exceptional women because they are rare. They stay calm under pressure, loyal in hardship, and grateful in plenty. They bring solutions instead of problems. They give more than they take.

Being exceptional does not mean being perfect. It means being accountable, self-aware, and willing to grow. It means standing out in a culture that rewards arrogance, chaos, and comfort. It is the quiet strength that separates a wife from a warning.

You do not have to be flawless. You just need to be consistent. The world is full of average people. Be the exception.

CASE STUDY

People magazine published an article about what happens when a wife is exceptional. Betty and Elton Denner are 100 and 101 years old and have been married for 82 years. This is only possible when an exceptional woman becomes an exceptional wife.

• • •

Learn from the Tenets

The tenets are not suggestions. They are survival skills. Men are not lining up to marry potential. They are looking for proof. Proof that you bring value, not entitlement. Proof that you can sacrifice, not demand. Proof that you can keep the chaos low enough for peace to survive. If you ignore the tenets, you will repeat the same mistakes, tell the same stories, and blame the same men. Follow them and you might shock yourself by becoming the exception. And if the word "exception" makes you roll your eyes, that tells the whole story.

The tenets work because they rebuild what modern culture has stripped away. They restore discipline, humility, and self-awareness. They teach you to pause before reacting, to listen before judging, and to value harmony more than victory. They move you away from performance and back toward character. When a woman starts living by these principles, men notice. Not because she is chasing them, but because she finally carries what most women have lost: calm, consistency, control. The tenets are not about perfection. They are about rarity.

These twenty principles will not guarantee a proposal next month, but they will change your trajectory. They will shift how men experience you. They will separate you from a crowd of women who all sound the same, behave the same, and repeat the same excuses. If you want marriage, this is how you prepare for it. If you want respect, this is how you earn it. If you want love that lasts, this is how you build it.

The women who take the tenets seriously rise. The women who ignore them stay lost. The difference is simple. One learns. The other repeats.

Why Men Won't Marry You

The End Is Near

• • •

No, marriage is not dying, but the rules of the marriage game have changed.

For decades, men were expected to play a rigged game and smile through the loss. Women were told they could have everything without giving anything. The result has not been empowerment. It has been loneliness.

Men are not doing anything new. They are doing what men have always done. They are adapting. When women turned dates into resource extraction, men stopped paying for dates. When wives repeatedly took half of a man's income, half of his assets, and half of his peace, men stopped getting married. Women may dislike that shift, but men are not required to volunteer for their own suffering.

Mike Tyson said it plainly: "Everyone has a plan until they get punched in the mouth." That lesson applies to relationships just as much as it does to boxing. Women can have plans. They can have demands. They can have lists of what they think they deserve. But the men they want might not choose them. Even when they do choose, a man can walk away at any time. Men get a vote. No one can force a man into marriage.

This book was never written to attack women or to praise men. It was written to expose the truth everyone sees but no one wants to say.

The 22 Truths exist because the patterns exist. They are not theories. They are behaviors. They are realities that repeated themselves until men eventually stopped arguing and started acting.

The reasons are not guilt trips. They are for your awareness. A woman cannot correct what she refuses to see, which is why the 20 Tenets exist. They are not commands. They are calibration points. They represent balance and reflect what men value, what women once instinctively understood, and what modern culture has drowned out.

If you felt anger while reading them, it means something inside you resisted the truth. If you felt conviction, it means part of you wants to grow. Men are not the enemy. Men are tired and cautious. They have seen what happens to naïve husbands, and they now choose silence over sacrifice. Women mistake that silence for oppression when it is simply self-protection.

The end is not near for marriage.

The end is near for denial!

The end is near for the fantasy that love can survive without respect, or that partnership can survive without humility.

If you can look in the mirror and accept your part in the story, you can change the entire story. You will begin to understand why men refuse marriage. Only then can you understand what may make a man consider marriage again. Men have not given up on love. They have given up on losing themselves to prove it.

The end of lies is near. The beginning starts when you finally tell the truth.

Men and women are not enemies. They are partners who lost the handbook. We traded wisdom for opinions and structure for comfort. We turned relationships into competitions, and both sides paid the price.

By reaching this point in the book, you already understand the 22 Truths and Why Men Will Not Marry You. Those truths are not insults. They are mirrors. Each one reflects habits, attitudes, and patterns modern women have been encouraged to adopt, even though they destroy the exact things they want.

The 20 Tenets should not be seen as restrictions. They are solutions. They were the blueprint that helped generations before us build homes, families, and loyalty. Understanding the 22 Truths and the 20 Tenets is how you will move forward.

Just keep some basic concepts in mind to help you move into your future relationships:

"Happy" Is Not a Foundation

Happiness is temporary. It shifts with emotion, timing, hormones, stress, and convenience. It cannot carry a marriage. If your entire relationship depends on staying "happy," then you will divorce the moment life becomes normal.

Women end marriages because they confuse comfort with emptiness. They confuse boredom with incompatibility. They confuse routine with failure. Men have been bored in marriage for thousands of years, yet they stay. Women feel bored for a month and file paperwork. Men now understand the risk.

Meeting Men Is Not Complicated

Good men are not extinct. They are quiet. They have watched the world change, and they have chosen caution over chaos. When you meet a man today, understand that he is guarded, not because he hates women, but because he has watched too many women quit when relationships stop feeling fun.

Respect gets through to him. Respect is not flattery. It involves being curious, listening, and giving him the benefit of the doubt instead of assuming he's participating in all of the worst parts of the Bible. Men open up around peaceful women, but they shut down when they feel pressure.

Approach him as an individual. Not as a symbol. Not as a replacement, or a project. He is in no way responsible for what the last man did to you. He is not a checklist or a supervillain waiting to attack you or your fragile sensibilities. He is someone who wants peace just as much as you do.

You Need to Rate Yourself Honestly

We discussed ratings because reality matters. Most people are average. Some are below average, while some are above average. That is life. And as such: Below-average men marry below average women. Average men marry average women; likewise, above-average men generally marry above-average women.

But as we discussed, women in every category dream of the top-tier men. They want the tall men with high incomes, who are fit, and look amazing. But those men rarely choose women who are not themselves amazing and fit. Think about it logically. Below average women and average women expect an above-average man. But the above-average man is looking for an above-average woman.

The below-average and average women can say they won't settle for less, but they do not seem to understand that, to an above-average man, he would be "settling for less" by settling for them.

If you overrate yourself, you eliminate yourself. Be realistic. It is the only way forward.

Dating With Purpose Is required
Dating is not a game to win. It is not a tournament or a spotlight for your highlight reel. Dating with purpose means you stop chasing the top 20% and start noticing the loyal men who actually want partnership.

Dating apps have done real damage. Women get attention simply for being women. That attention turns into confusion. Women mistake male access for male desire. Men are not picky on apps. They are opportunistic. Being approached does not make you valuable. It makes you available.

Communicate clearly. Speak calmly. Disagree respectfully. You can be strong without being harsh. You can be assertive without being combative. A feminine woman knows how to disagree without creating war.

Don't Speak to Men Like You're Crazy
Men respond to respect. Not volume. Not accusation. Not dramatics. Speak clearly, not emotionally. Men listen to clarity. They ignore chaos. Men do not accuse women of womansplaining (or she-laborating). They simply walk away. They choose peace over conflict every time.

No man likes a "crazy" woman. It is the one thing they fear. If a man can sense that you are crazy before they find themselves in a relationship with you, that relationship will never grow.

Every conversation a man has with you reveals whether you are a partner or an opponent. In man speak, **are you for a long-time... or are you for a fun-time?** You don't want to be a "fun-time" girl. *You want to be a "long time" girl!* A man will keep you around for years because he's having fun and loving you. But, if he's not interested in marrying you, is that a good thing for you? Probably not. Choose wisely if you want to marry that man.

Rebuild the Natural Balance

The world changed, but nature did not. Masculine men still desire feminine women. Feminine women still desire masculine men. That balance is not oppression. It is order and harmony. The men you want demand respect, appreciation, loyalty, femininity, clear communication, effort, and stability. A woman who brings these, quite simply, will be chosen every time... over a loud, masculine, aggressive woman.

Marriage will return, but not for everyone. It will return for the women who learned from the wreckage marriage currently is and those who drop the background noise and abandon inflated ego and pride. Marriage will come for those who have rebuilt themselves with calm, clarity, and purpose.

It is important to understand that strength without humility becomes arrogance and independence without gratitude will become loneliness. But when you recognize that women are more affected by loneliness, you understand who will be affected the most. That is **you**!

The Final Verdict

You do not need to apologize for wanting love. You only need to prepare yourself for it. Learn how men think. Respect what they value. Speak to them as allies instead of adversaries. Live the 20 Tenets until they become instinct and remember the 22 Truths not as insults, but as reminders of how quickly peace can be destroyed.

The end of this book is not the end of hope. It is the end of pretending. It is the end of believing that a relationship can thrive without structure, that respect is optional, or that accountability does not matter. Peace only exists where truth is allowed.

When you choose honesty over ego and cooperation over rebellion, you position yourself for the kind of love that endures. You attract a man who sees you as a partner he can finally build with instead of another opponent he must protect himself from.

If you understand the lessons in *Why Men Will Not Marry You*, you will see that the problem is rarely the men. It is usually one of three things. Either:

1. No one taught you how men actually think.
2. You believed only a woman's perspective mattered, or
3. You don't care what men think.

If you don't care what men think, then no one can really help you get yourself married. You're hopeless!

But if you want to get married, you no longer have the excuse that no one taught you how men think. If you only thought a woman's perspective mattered, hopefully now you understand—that if no one is pleased with you or your behavior, no man has to wife you up.

With this book, at least you have the truth in your hands.

Just understand that men have not changed nearly as much as women choose to believe. Marriage, family, and legacy are still priorities for most men. But modern men will not allow themselves to be victimized by women or the system that punishes them for marriage.

Men's acceptance of marital risk has taken a dive. They will marry, but to achieve it, they will demand loyalty, peace, gratitude, and purpose. They still want a woman who brings stability rather than stress. Men are no longer willing to sacrifice everything for a woman who brings only herself but demands the world.

If you have reached this final page, you already know the truth as men experience it. Not the filtered version, not the emotional version, but the version that reality continues to prove.

The question is simple. Will you accept this information?

That choice is yours.

No. Marriage is not dead! The delusion around it is. The women who accept reality, embrace accountability, and live by the tenets will stand out in a world where chaos is common and peace is rare. You do not need perfection to be chosen. You need humility, consistency, and the willingness to grow. The truth has been laid out clearly. What you do with it now will determine the love you attract and the future you create.

Pinckney House Publishing

www.ingramcontent.com/pod-product-compliance
Lightning Source LLC
Chambersburg PA
CBHW060524100426
42743CB00009B/1429